Wild Words/
Dangerous Desires

Studies in the
Postmodern Theory of Education

Joe L. Kincheloe and Shirley R. Steinberg
General Editors

Vol. 64

PETER LANG
New York • Washington, D.C./Baltimore • Boston • Bern
Frankfurt am Main • Berlin • Brussels • Vienna • Oxford

Helen J. Harper

Wild Words/ Dangerous Desires

High School Girls and Feminist Avant-Garde Writing

PETER LANG
New York • Washington, D.C./Baltimore • Boston • Bern
Frankfurt am Main • Berlin • Brussels • Vienna • Oxford

Library of Congress Cataloging-in-Publication Data

Harper, Helen J.
Wild words/dangerous desires: high school girls
and feminist avant-garde writing / Helen J. Harper.
p. cm. — (Counterpoints; v. 64)
Includes bibliographical references.
1. Creative writing (Secondary education)—Case studies. 2. Feminist
literature—Study and teaching (Secondary)—Case studies. 3. Literature,
Experimental—Study and teaching (Secondary)—Case studies.
4. Teenage girls—Education—Case studies. I. Title. II. Series:
Counterpoints (New York, N.Y.); vol. 64.
LB1631.H267   808'.042'0712—DC21   97-21411
ISBN 0-8204-3861-8
ISSN 1058-1634

Die Deutsche Bibliothek-CIP-Einheitsaufnahme

Harper, Helen J.:
Wild words/dangerous desires: high school girls
and feminist avant-garde writing / Helen J. Harper.
–New York; Washington, D.C./Baltimore; Boston; Bern;
Frankfurt am Main; Berlin; Brussels; Vienna; Oxford: Lang.
(Counterpoints; Vol. 64)
ISBN 0-8204-3861-8

Cover design by Nona Reuter

The paper in this book meets the guidelines for permanence and durability
of the Committee on Production Guidelines for Book Longevity
of the Council of Library Resources.

Printed in the United States of America

to my mother,
of course

Acknowledgements

The introductory chapter to this text is entitled "Letting Wildness into the Words." I am deeply indebted to those who have given me the courage to let wildness into my words in and beyond the confines of academic life. My thanks to my parents, Nadia and Ken Gray, my brothers, their wives, and especially to my grandmother, Phyllis Harper; also to John Willinsky who started me in this work with his energy and enthusiasm for academic life; to a group of brilliant and passionate young scholars: Holly Baines, Nombuso Dlamini, Bonny Norton, Alice Pitt, Judith Robertson, Arleen Schenke, Anita Sheth, Meagan Terepocki, Andrew Thornton, Rinaldo Walcott, Tony Xerri, and Elizabeth Yeoman, who have challenged and supported me intellectually through many years of graduate study. In particular I extend my appreciation to Handel Kashope Wright. My gratitude as well to friends Kathleen Troy, Terese Truchan, LaDonna MacRae; and to Martin Hansen for his good humour, long phone calls and unrelenting support. More recently I have been encouraged in the last stages of research by Shirley Steinberg and Joe Kincheloe and by my colleagues at the Faculty of Education, University of Western Ontario. And of course there is Marshall, with whom I celebrate love and life every single day. To Marshall, to my family, to my friends, and comrades all, thank you.

Of course I am deeply grateful to the young women who participated in what was a more difficult study than any of us had anticipated. And to Roger Simon, my academic advisor, I extend my deepest appreciation for his intelligent and compassionate support, and his belief that pedagogy can make a difference.

The poem "The Thesis Proposal (a draft)" that opens Chapter One was originally published in *Resources for Feminist Research,* vol. 2, nos. 3 + 4, (Fall/Winter, 1992), pp. 14-15. Reprinted by permission of the publisher. All rights reserved. An earlier version of Chapter Seven was published in Sharon Todd's (1997) *Learning Desire: Perspectives on Pedagogy, Culture and the Unsaid,* London: Routledge. Every effort has been made to secure permission for copyrighted material used in this text. Any inquiries should be directed to the publisher or author.

Table of Contents

Introduction:

Letting Wildness Into the Words

It was hard to leave that country, that clean land. Hard to find a way
into the impure, no longer so clearly centred, confusing modern world.
Hard to find words for this wild journey. Hard to become a writer,
committing perjury all the time against the sacred Book. Letting the
wildness into the words. Transgressing, remembering the old fear.
Listening to the earth and the women, breathless with desire, wanting
so much the dance and the laughter, the unholy babble of speech.

(Di Brandt, *(f.)Lip*, 1988)

This book is about identity, desire, and writing. It concerns the
struggles of young women to define themselves with and against the
subject positions made available to them in school reading and
writing practices, and what ultimately sanctions or encourages certain
positionings. It is based on a study—my study—of six high school
girls who were given an opportunity to transgress conventional school
writing practices—to let wildness into their words—using feminist
avant-garde literature as support. I was interested in what students
might produce given the chance to break convention, and what such
an opportunity would mean in terms of a feminist agenda. What
quickly became apparent was that to read and produce (or not) "wild
writing" using feminist avant-garde literature was not an easy task.
The experience required the young women to negotiate the set of
premises, practices, and pleasures that mark the female subject in
feminist avant-garde literature. And these negotiations were not easy.
Confronting an alternative conception of "woman" both exposed
and threatened the intellectual and affective structures that supported

more familiar senses of themselves as women, students, readers, and writers within school discourses. The experience also challenged my own sense of myself as a feminist and as a teacher. The disturbing or unsettling moments brought about by the "wild words" of the feminist avant-garde exposed much about identification and desire produced with and against school texts, and the possibilities for a feminist pedagogy that might work with these processes.

The act of disturbing taken-for-granted assumptions and con-ventional practices lies at the heart of feminist avant-garde writing and feminist pedagogy. Such action is informed by a larger project of challenging the ways in which gender as a social and discursive construct, together with other constructs (e.g., race, class, ethnicity), shape and limit the range of identities possible for women. Effective intervention into these processes is dependent on understanding the social and psychological organization of gender identity; more gen-erally, to know the intellectual and affective scaffolding that supports and limits who one can be and who one wishes to be. What has become increasingly clear is that desire and identification are key to this scaffolding, that is, to the structuring of identity.

It is argued from the perspective of psychoanalytic theory that who one wishes to be (identification) and who one wishes to have (desire) organise a play of difference and similitude in self-other relations that mark the boundaries of a recognisable identity (Fuss, 1995). The sharp edges of similitude and difference form boundaries that provide a necessary sense of self from which actions are directed. However, the delineation of a self can be limiting in that it demands the exclusion or expulsion of other possibilities. Femininity, for example, in the binaries of Western thought has been organised to include emotionality and to exclude rationality.

For feminist pedagogy the central question or task is finding the most effective form of pedagogical intervention in the play of similitude and difference that would break open the range of identities possible. How do we intervene effectively, using the power of identification, in a project of social transformation? For those who work with female adolescents and/or their teachers, what pedagogical intervention might best serve young women now and as adults? The study described in this book explored one rather dramatic attempt at intervention into the school reading and writing experiences of young women.

Identity and Identification
in School Reading and Writing Practices

As a former high school English teacher, I am interested in school literacy practices as a site for social and personal transformation. Acts of literacy have come to be understood, not as something transposed onto our lives, but as a lived experience that can affirm or disrupt understandings of self and the world. More particularly, reading can offer moments of identification with character, setting, and theme that allow for the reorganisation of similitude and difference between self and other. Identification involves a recognition of similarity: "I am like you." As a psychological process, the recognition of similarity is possible because an individual has, at some point, assimilated an aspect of "the other," and, as a result, has been transformed wholly or partially. An individual can see herself in a character, and indeed becomes that character, having incorporated some aspect of the character as part of herself.

Psychoanalytic theory suggests that what prompts identification is a loss of human relatedness, specifically the loss of love objects (S. Freud, 1964a). As Diana Fuss has described it, identification is a process of substitution and displacement: an ordinary process of "installing surrogate others to fill the void where we imagine love objects to have been" (1995, p. 1). We attempt to replace internally what is missing externally. Since reading requires incorporating words on a page into one's experience and understanding of the world, the possibilities for intense identification are always present. Indeed identification as a specific psychological process may be a necessary component of our richest reading experiences. Our favourite books—those we obsess about, reading and rereading, for example, may be those in which intense identification has occurred. Perhaps what reading offers us is a vehicle for identification: one means of compensating for loss.

Adolescence can be defined in terms of change and loss. Obviously there is the loss of childhood. Anna Freud (1971) suggested that changes in sexual impulses at puberty necessitate a shift from the former love objects of childhood (parents and siblings) to others outside the family. Culture also plays a crucial role. In Western society, for example, young adults often leave or are encouraged to leave the family home. Whether socially or psychologically organised, there is a profound, albeit at times exhilarating, loss of connection with parents and a search for substitutes. Thus intense identification as an act of substitution may be a central feature of adolescent experience generally and of adolescent reading experience specifically.

For young women the rupture between childhood and adolescence involves not only the loss of connection with parents, but also a loss of connection with Western society more generally. Language is key to this loss. Drawing on the work of Jacques Lacan, Cora Kaplan (1991) suggests that language is key in gender identity and becomes particularly problematic and unsettling for female adolescents. For Lacan, the acquisition of language is what turns subjects into human and social beings, but entry into the symbolic order is organised differently for females than for males. According to Kaplan, in the Oedipal phase identification with the mother requires a young girl to accept as permanent the missing phallus. Since language is produced in patriarchy such that the phallus is the crucial signifier, a woman's relationship to language is organised negatively, or at least eccentrically. At puberty, when adult sexuality is negotiated, there is a reinscription of gender identity played out partly in terms of one's relationship to language first organised in the Oedipal stage.

Kaplan maintains that in Western culture women's different or negative relation is expressed in, among other things, the taboo against women's public speech. While this taboo has been challenged, it nonetheless continues to exert a powerful influence on women's lives and identities. For women, "the very condition of their accession to their own subjectivity, to the consciousness of a self which is both personal and public is their unwitting acceptance of the law which limits their speech. This condition places them in a special relation to language which becomes theirs as a consequence of being human, and at the same time not theirs as a consequence of becoming female" (Kaplan, 1991, p. 68). Although there has been considerable feminist debate about traditional Freudian theory and its "missing phallus," what is important here is that Kaplan points to a crucial connection between gender identity and language in relation to adolescent girls.

From another perspective, Carol Gilligan (1990), in a study of girls' psychological development, describes a more general loss, or more precisely, a problem of connection to Western culture that all women, but in particular young women face:

Perhaps adolescence is an especially critical time in women's development because it poses a problem of connection that is not easily
resolved. As the river of a girl's life flows in to the sea of Western
culture she is in danger of drowning or disappearing. To take on the
problem of appearance, which is the problem of her development,
and to connect her life with history on a cultural scale, she must
enter—and by entering disrupt—a tradition in which "human" has for
the most part meant male. (p. 4)

Barbara Hudson (1984) suggests that the difficulties young
women experience arise from the incompatibility of discourses on
femininity and adolescence:

Femininity and adolescence as discourses [are] subversive of each other.
All of our images of the adolescent—the restless, searching teen; the
Hamlet figure; the sower of wild oats and tester of growing
powers—these are masculine figures. . .If adolescence is characterised
by masculine constructs, then any attempt by girls to satisfy society's
demands of them qua adolescents is bound to involve them in displaying notably a lack of maturity but also a lack of femininity. (p. 35)

Finding it difficult to reconcile such differences, young women,
indeed all women (particularly those marginalised by race, class, ethnicity, and sexual orientation) struggle to keep from disappearing in
Western culture, from having no identity, or, as suggested by Luce
Irigaray (1977), from identifying with absence.

Poststructural theory suggests that absence and presence are organised through discourses—sets of social meanings and practices,
including language and literary practices. Discourses provide subject
positions or "ways to be" present or absent in the world. Thus, girls
become "girls" by participating within those available sets of discourses that define them as "girls" (Weedon, 1997; Jones, 1997,
1993). Although there are multiple and competing discourses, relations of power organise or promote particular social meanings and
practices, and thus, particular subject positions. This is accomplished
largely through a process of normalisation or naturalisation wherein a
discourse and the subject positions it constitutes so dominate a
particular institution that all others are suppressed. It becomes natural
and legitimate. The subject position it offers becomes the way of
being, and what is most available as a source for identification.

As feminists have long pointed out, traditional discursive practices both in and outside of school contexts are limited in the "ways of being" they offer girls and young women. Research over the last twenty years reveals the myriad of ways in which girls are disadvantaged in school contexts. Research indicates that teacher behaviour and specific school policies and practices (including access to courses and programs as well as the specific content of subjects and lessons) often reinforce gender stereotypes (AAUW, 1995; Gaskell and McLaren, 1989; Spender and Sarah, 1980; Deem, 1980). Studies have revealed girls' relative silence in classrooms, their overrepresentation in certain curriculum areas, their lack of role models, and their lack of achievement in particular subjects (Sadker and Sadker, 1994; Middleton and Jones, 1992; Gaskell and McLaren, 1989). Recent research also finds that incidents of sexual harassment and physical violence are a part of school experience for many girls and young women (Larkin, 1997, 1994; Stein, Marshall, and Tropp, 1993).

In terms of school literacy practices, studies have pointed to the limited number of literary texts written by women, the stereotyping of male and female characters, the teaching of phallocentric reading strategies, and the particular policing of girls' writing (Sadker and Sadker, 1994; Gilbert, 1992, 1989b, 1988; Barnes, 1990; Caywood and Overing, 1987; Annas, 1985; Frith, 1981; Galloway, 1980; Farrell, 1979; Fetterley, 1978). In general there is a limited number of powerful subject positions from which girls can read or write; a limited number of possibilities for identification with femininity as an active, powerful, and present force (Davies and Banks, 1992; Gilbert, 1992, 1989b). For example, Pam Gilbert found in her study of ten-year-old girls that they experienced difficulty constructing stories and subject positions that lay outside discourses that constructed women as subordinate. Gilbert (1989b) noted that the female characters in the girls' stories

> ended up being tied to marriage, fidelity, and female dependence on male protection. When they [the girls] tried to write about independence, they instead wrote about male erosion of their independence. When they tried to write about women on their own, they wrote about daughters and fiancees. . . The girls resisted the inevitability of marriage, physical domination and restricted freedom, but they had no speaking positions of authority available to them, no alternative discourses which offered them other ways of constructing the feminine.   (pp. 262–263)

Educators have, of course, responded to this particular kind of criticism and feminist criticism of schooling more generally. Working from a perspective that young women are socialised into sex roles, many teachers in the 1970s and 1980s supplemented curricula with materials that offered a greater range of roles for women and young girls. Attempts have been made to include more texts by women, stories with stronger female characters, and in general more nonsexist print and non-print materials. Although the perspective is different, this study, in exploring the possibilities of feminist avant-garde as alternative literary material, can be seen as part of an effort to provide alternative subject positions and alternative possibilities for identification.

Feminist Avant-Garde Literature

Feminist avant-garde literature is a form of insurgent writing. It is constituted by a set of textual practices, premises, and pleasures that transgress language and literary convention. Experimentation with lexicon, syntax, genre form, plot structure, image, and theme is highly valued, done in the name of a feminist politics by women writers. Virginia Woolf, George Sand, Djuna Barnes, and, in the Canadian context, Nicole Brossard, Daphne Marlett, Betsy Warland, Beth Brant, and Marlene Nourbese Philip, are among those who are often cited as working within the genre of feminist avant-garde writing.[1]

The promise of this genre is that literary and language experimentation will unsettle or disrupt the symbolic order, destabilising gender identity and identification, and so creating a space to expand possibilities for imaging the world and one's place in the world. Feminist avant-garde writing also provides an example of a community of women writers, readers, and publishers intent on reworking and rewriting women's place in the world. This community produces and stabilises an active presence for women writers not easily negotiated in other contexts. The writing and the workings of this literary community offer young women alternative and perhaps better possibilities for organising a sense of themselves as women writers and readers.

Although there has been a resurgence in feminist avant-garde writing over the last ten years as a result of renewed political energy and interest in poststructural theories of language, this resurgence has been largely confined to academic and leftist literary circles. The importance and potential of feminist avant-garde writing is not widely recognised generally, nor is it necessarily welcomed. In conjunction with feminism, the disruptive and subversive nature of this particular literary formation can be seen as a potential threat to the established practices and meanings that constitute social institutions, such as the family, the church, the school, and the legal system. If schools are understood as places of cultural transmission, where the young are given the knowledge, skills, and identities that name and authorise status quo notions of human possibility, then literary work that disrupts that process is hardly going to be viewed as particularly useful or appropriate.

But even if schools are viewed as places for expanding the range of who one can be, various other discourses make such a project difficult. For example, although English literature and/or Language Arts class would seem an ideal site for students to examine the discursive formation of identity and identification, its potential has largely been undermined by pedagogical discourses firmly grounded in psychology, progressivism, and humanism (Morgan, 1993; O'Neill, 1992; Gilbert 1991, 1989a). These discourses are limited in their ability to address identity and identification in part because they assume implicitly and explicitly that language and literary practices are ideologically innocent: acting only as a transparent medium that reflects a preexisting reality. This preexisting reality includes a fixed, stable, and knowable self or personality that can be discovered. Reading and writing are viewed as tools that operate to provide insight into this reality and into one's self. In the case of girls and young women, reading and writing are tools to discover the "real" girl or young woman within, rather than as acts that themselves produce or construct what it means to be a girl or young woman.

These premises fail to acknowledge shifts in language and meaning, and most importantly, fail to acknowledge the politics affecting these shifts. It is important to understand how language and literary practices work to produce a reading of the world and one's self in order to intervene in and expand the range of identities possible for girls. Until English/Language Arts pedagogy addresses language as a social, semiotic sign central in the formation of identity, English/LA Studies classrooms will be limiting places for young women. And avant-garde writing, and in particular feminist avant-garde writing, where language is never taken-for-granted, never transparent, never outside of relations of power, will not be easily entertained.

Pedagogical discourses are not the only difficulty. In general adolescent girls are not particularly enamored by the discourses of feminism or by feminist avant-garde writing. In reviewing " Talk Sixteen," a film documentary about the lives of five sixteen-year-old girls, the author noted that the young women viewed feminism not simply as irrelevant in their lives but as something quite repulsive:

> They related to the word "feminism" like a slug that had just crawled into their French fries. And they were typical, because with very few exceptions, the other 350 teenagers who auditioned for Talk 16 were as clueless or negative about feminism. *(Globe and Mail*, February 10, 1993, p. A16)

But even if an education in feminism was provided so that students were not clueless or negative about the topic, there is a host of other problems with securing any alternative discourse, let alone a literary formation like feminist avant-garde writing. What is more and more obvious is that the mere presence of an alternative discourse does not necessarily make it "available" as a resource for self-reconstitution: as a site for identification. This availability problem is something I remember from my own teaching experience.

The "Availability" Problem

Like other educators of the 1980s, I sought to extend "ways of being female" for my students by increasing the number of texts by women in my classroom, and by extending the range of writing topics through the creation of curricular spaces for "freewriting." I also advocated the use of gender-sensitive language and took special efforts to encourage girls in academic pursuits and career choices. I actively discouraged romance reading in my classroom and fought with librarians to get such literature removed from the school library, thinking that this genre was responsible for lulling my students into accepting traditional marriages and more specifically, into viewing passive and dependent behavior as legitimate and desirable. As well I saw myself, as a single career woman, working on a male-dominated teaching staff, as a role model to my young women students who lived in a small town that offered few other models. I am now somewhat embarrassed by the naivete of these attempts. It is perhaps not surprising that my efforts and those of others were largely unsuccessful. The girls I taught reproduced traditional patterns of thinking and behavior in my class and, as much as I know, in their adult lives, with no more insight into the process by which this happened than I had into my own conformity. Indeed, as I think of it now, there were perhaps more serious ramifications. By exposing students to more choices, the girls' decision (with rare exception) to confine themselves to conventional patterns seemed to confirm to me, perhaps to my students, and certainly to others, an essentialised notion of femininity—that maybe when all was said and done that was just "the way girls are." Although I would hotly contest this publicly, in the privacy of my own thoughts I often wondered.

My attempts at intervention and the doubts that emerged were, in retrospect, predictable. The work was based on the assumption that a wider range of more powerful subject positions would become instantly available to girls exposed to feminist practices and materials. However, the process by which girls "become girls" (or more generally individuals become subjects) is far more complex than what I and others had believed. The power of dominant discourses is not so easily routed.

As mentioned earlier, dominant discourse structures what subject positions are considered natural, normal, and legitimate—something quite difficult to counteract, as noted by Alison Jones (1993):

> Girls perceive (in their wide observations from media, family, everyday life) the positions—including the silences—available to "normal" women, and usually regulate their own desires and behaviours within those parameters. This is not simply false consciousness which can be altered with some feminist education; it is not a choice between being liberated and being oppressed. Rather it is a choice between being "okay" or "normal" and being "weird," between being on the margins or in the centres—albeit the marginalised centres reserved for women. (p. 162)

Similarly, Bronwyn Davies (1989) has noted in her research of feminist fairy tales that young girls do not necessarily read alternative female subject positions as desirable. Davies found that some preschoolers reading the feminist fairy tale "Paper Bag Princess" saw the princess, an active and heroic character who in the end refuses to marry the prince, not as daring and admirable, but as unattractive and unfortunate. This character, according to some of the children, could not be considered "a real princess" because in light of the narrative available within the dominant discourses on princesses and feminine behavior, she was weird—someone who got things just a bit wrong. The possibility of being strong, autonomous, and a princess, was a position offered by the text, but not available to the students.

Part of what sanctions a particular position as legitimate (or not) and so available or not, is our memories of previous subject positioning, or discursive interpellations.[2] Interpellation is the process whereby an individual is turned into a subject. Louis Althusser (1971) described the process:

> I shall then suggest that ideology "acts" or "functions" in such a way that it "recruits" subjects among the individuals (it recruits them all), or transforms the individuals into subjects (it transform them all) by that very precise operation which I have called interpellation or hailing, and which can be imagined along the lines of the most commonplace everyday police (or other) hailing: "Hey, you there!" (pp. 162–163)

In this process individuals are not passively shaped by the actions of others; rather, they actively take up as their own, the discourses through which they are shaped—they answer the hail. In doing so individuals mistakenly take themselves to be the authors of their own subjectivity. Thus discourses and their subject positions are not seen as something to be wary of or to be challenged. The strength of this belief makes it difficult to disrupt previous interpellations.

Discourses organise not only our cognitive life but also our affective experiences—our desires and pleasures—which in turn constitute and support particular identities. As Peter McLaren (1991) describes, "Discourses do not sit on the surface of the flesh nor float about in the formless ether of the mind but are enfolded into the very structures of our desire inasmuch as desire itself is formed by the anonymous historical rules of 'discourse'" (p. 154). The memories of previous interpellations include memories of past pleasures and desires that are inscribed onto the body. We become invested affectively as well as intellectually in a particular discourse; that is, we are organised emotionally and intellectually in what is deemed the natural and legitimate way of understanding and defining ourselves. In an important article, Bronwyn Davies (1990) carefully connects desire and discourse:

> Desire is spoken into existence. It is shaped through discursive and interactive practices, through the symbolic and semiotic. Desires are constituted through the narratives and storylines, the metaphors, the very language and patterns of existence through which we are "interpellated" into the social world. . . . [Desire is] implicated in our interpretation of ourselves and of others. (p. 501]

If our affective investments or commitments are produced or at least organised in narratives and storylines, it is important to examine what is being created for/by the reader. Valerie Walkerdine's (1987) analysis of preteen comics as well as Angela McRobbie's (1992) work on the adolescent magazine *Jackie* demonstrates how culture products for girls organise particular desires and subject positions for young women. Walkerdine and McRobbie both suggest that fiction and fantasy operate on a symbolic level to map onto the struggles in girls' lives, offering and organising desires and pleasures. In the case of the comics and the *Jackie* magazine, heterosexuality—Mr. Right, the Prince—are offered as the solution to girls' problems. This affective investment organises and connects reader to the subject position on offer—teenaged girl as defined through heterosexual desire and her search for Mr. Right.

But there is more at work in reading and writing practices. As stated previously reading can offer opportunities for intense identification. The power of which is captured by Kingsley Amis in a quotation about the popular movie character James Bond. Amis writes, "We don't want to have Bond to dinner or to go golfing with Bond or talk to Bond. We want to *be* Bond" (Bennett and Woollacott, 1987, p. 204). Our identifications provide compensation for a psychological (if not actual) loss securing a powerful connection or incorporation of "the other" into ourselves, which at least for a time may offer comfort, pleasure, and/or relief. Diane Fuss comments, "Identifications are the origin of some of our most powerful, enduring, and deeply felt pleasures," the memories of which may secure us in powerful ways to character, or, more generally, a subject position (1995, p. 2).

Considering all of this, it does not seem likely or even possible that alternative discourses and alternative subject positions (feminist or otherwise) would ever be easily or instantly available. Fortunately, for those who seek to expand the range of possible identities beyond those few authorised, identification as a psychic process connecting us to what has been lost is never entirely successful, never entirely satisfactory (Butler, 1993, 1990). In part this is because what is incorporated into our notion of ourselves is only ever a facsimile of "the other," not the real thing. Furthermore, identifications are thought to be mobile and elastic, shifting and changing, disappearing and appearing as our psychic and social lives demand. If the process of identification that organises similitude and difference, naming and substantiating identity, is so dynamic, then identity can never be permanently secured. It can be unmoored.

Furthermore, the power a discourse, and the possible identificatory moments it offers, can be disrupted and resisted since there are always multiple and counter discourses at play in any moment. But even if there were only one dominant discourse in operation, the very naming and structuring of a discourse and its preferred subject position(s) implies alternatives, even if alternative discourses are not in circulation, that is, not articulated or practiced. Indeed, alternative modes of knowledge, and subject positions and their attendant pleasures and desires are made possible by the power of a dominant discourse. Foucault wrote,"Discourse transmits and produces power; it reinforces it but it also undermines and exposes it, renders it fragile and makes it possible to thwart it. In like manner, silence and secrecy are a shelter for power, anchoring its prohibitions, but they also loosen its hold and provide for relatively obscure areas of tolerances" (1981, p. 10). Alternative modes of intelligence, emotionality, desire pleasure, and, ultimately, alternative discourses and subject positions are always there, waiting in the wings. Resistance and change are always possible.

Yet while potential alternatives may be ready and waiting, the question remains how and when an alternative discourse and its subject positions become or do not become available. In other words, when can other identifications be entertained, and at what cost. It is important to understand what is at play in transformative moments when identities and identifications are destabilised. More practically, any attempt to expand the range of identities available to girls and young women require understanding what is at stake in their struggles with and against what is offered. As part of such work, this book explores how young women students struggle with and against the subject positions, more specifically the identificatory possibilities, offered in feminist avant-garde writing, and most importantly what intellectual and affective investments underpin these struggles.

Investments are the commitments produced within discourses that connect an individual to a subject position, directing his or her emotions, thoughts, and energies (Grossberg, 1986). This book explores what affective and intellectual investments seem to secure (or not) identification with the subject positions offered in feminist avant-garde writing. This research then examines the negotiations of a group of young women with the premises, pleasures, and practices of feminist avant-garde writing in their talk and in their expository and most importantly in their creative writing to determine what affective and intellectual investments encourage or sanction particular subject positionings. As stated at the outset of this chapter, this work analyzes how and why students embrace or refuse the woman created in feminist avant-garde writing. This is done from a feminist perspective, with the ultimate goal of expanding the range of identities available to young women.

What follows is divided into seven chapters. The first chapter describes the background and promise of feminist writing practices, and the particular configuration of feminist avant-garde writing articulated within feminist literary journals at the time of the study. In effect this chapter provides an indication of what would seem to be on offer in this literary formation in terms of writing and reading practices and the subject position of "woman" constituted by those practices. The second chapter describes the "scene of writing," that is, the conditions and circumstances of the study. It delineates notions of writing as acts of composition, and further defines notions of investment, identification, and desire used in this text. The five chapters that follow focus on findings and implications of the study. Four of the chapters are organised by the responses of the students. There were six students in total and sufficient data to warrant separate chapters for Rebecca, Thea, and Janet. Data on the other three students, Denise, Lauren, and Zandra, are combined into a single chapter.[3] The concluding chapter outlines the themes that emerged across the participants. It also analyzes the implications of the findings with regard to theoretical and practical issues concerning identity, desire, and writing; the role and nature of feminist pedagogy; and the place of avant-garde literature in the education of young women.

Chapter One

Feminist Writing Practices: Wild Women/Wild Words

Thesis Proposal (draft)

So i sit down this morning to write,
having pushed my arm
across the kitchen table,
clearing away much of the bits and pieces
        of my life
creating a writing space/time
And fearing its loss,
i press my arm tight against the table top,
damming back those bits and pieces
        that may yet threaten

And with my free hand,
in my best handwriting,
on a new page, in my new scribbler
"I" write *Thesis Proposal*
 Finding those words a bit scary,
i add *(draft)*

i then pull out from my filing cabinet
a cardboard box—
a handout from a course taken and forgotten
 years ago
a typewritten, stapled, Xeroxed sheet
informing me of "elements normally
included in a thesis proposal"
i read:

"1. Nature of a Proposal

The proposal is a statement of the contract between
the student and his advisor (or his advisory committee
for a Ph.D.) either as it stands or in a modified form.
A thesis or dissertation is a report of research telling
of the problem, method, and results. The purpose of
the report is to inform the reader, not convince him of
the virtues of the research and should be written so
that the reader may reach his own conclusions
regarding the adequacy of the research and the validity
of the results and generalizations.

2. The Problem

These section normally includes:
     a) A brief introduction to the problem with
which the study is concerned. This may touch on
the theoretical basis or rationale for the problem and
show the place of the problem on the educational
scene.
     b) The statement of the problem *(in one or two
sentences)*
     c) The purpose of the study. This may include
the research questions or hypothesis. Sub-problems
should be precise and include implications for testing.
     d) Definition of the technical terms used or the
meaning given to key terms. Definitions should be
in operational terms and should be justified to the
reader."

i noticed in the margin of the page
i had drawn a flower

So returning to my new page, in my new scribbler
under *Thesis Proposal (draft)*
i write
Introduction: The Problem
and i stop.

On the farm, kids, even girls,
wear thick, black, orange-banded rubber boots
from mid-March to November.
There's a lot of freedom in rubber boots,
a lot of fun, particularly in spring.
But there's this moment in every kid's life
when the mud in the ditch rises significantly higher than
the boot tops
when something cold, and wet, and thick, oozes
down the inside of your boot,
down your warm, wool socks
and you know you are stuck—
and you feel it in your boots
and somehow in your guts

And some times in your cunt.

Cunt—I used to hate the word
but reading it in some woman's poem
I started to like it—something defiant about it.
Then I read it aloud to some man
who questioned my comfort with
"such a word"
And I said it again—Cunt
in *his* language
and started thrashing around inside, angry
what should I call it—listing other names,
all the while knowing
no name exists
in a voice i recognize
even
for my own body
in a language
I thought
was mine.

Thesis Proposal (draft)
Introduction: The Problem: Cunt
(in one or two sentences)

"The Problem" in One or Two Sentences

I begin this chapter with a poem of mine that speaks both to the difficulty I experienced in writing the proposal for this research and to the more general problem that women face whenever they write: the failure of dominant language practices to reflect or serve the interests, perspectives, and experiences of women. In this chapter I will discuss in greater detail the issue of women and language and the promise of feminist avant-garde literature, including a description of the practices, premises, and pleasures that mark "woman" as "she" is generally configured in Canadian feminist literary journals published in the 1990s. It is this "woman," and her identificatory possibilities that the teenagers worked with and against in this study. But before describing this woman, I will begin with "the problem" in slightly more than one or two sentences.

The problem of women and language, depicted rather more graphically in the poem, is certainly not new to research or to women writers. Over the last twenty-five years, feminist scholarship in language and literary criticism has revealed how gendered relations of power are reflected in and produced by conventional language practices. This work, in concert with theoretical and empirical studies in general linguistics, has effectively challenged the idea that language is politically neutral, and instead posited language as a form of social practice imbued with ideology.

Research has made apparent three political aspects of the relationship between women and language: first, women's use of language has and continues to be channeled into specific forms and locations that are often less directly powerful, economically, socially, and politically; secondly, that conventions and protocols of reading, writing, and speaking misrepresent or fail to represent women and their experiences; and thirdly, that the structure and lexicon of language itself can be shown to erase or devalue women.[1]

Research exploring the channels or limits placed on women's use of language has focused on the issue of women's silence in the public sphere. In Western societies historically, women's voices have been absent in the areas of law, literature, religion, politics, science, and technology. In part, this silence has been attributed to social traditions and taboos that restrict or limit women to the domestic sphere and to personal forms of language usage: for example, letters, diaries, journals, and gossip; as opposed to public sites and the often more prestigious and powerful forms of language, such as sermons, lectures, decrees, and editorials. This segregation has meant prohibiting or restricting women's access to formal education and thus to the literacy required of positions in the public domain. Of course there have been times when individual women or groups of women have gained access to powerful public positions, and there are and have been cultures in which women have held some degree of social and linguistic power, but such experiences are far from common. The category of woman, like that of child or slave, has been defined by the voicelessness in the public domain. One is, by definition legitimately a woman, or one could say recognizable as a woman, often by silence. Actual women who do have a voice in the public domain have been and often continue to be seen as aberrant, as not quite women, not quite feminine, not quite right.

It is important to acknowledge that men have acted individually and collectively as gatekeepers of language practices in their formal capacities as editors, administrators, adjudicators, and teachers, as well as in their roles as fathers, brothers, and husbands. It is also important to acknowledge that women (like men) caught within the hegemony of patriarchal discourse regulate themselves, each other, and their children, linguistically. But individuals (men and women alike) have also resisted, challenged, and circumvented the rules, traditions, and customs that have restricted women's access to certain language practices. Some of the more obvious rules of exclusion have been successfully challenged, allowing greater opportunity for women, albeit more often white, middle and upper-class women, to speak and write in the public sphere, to attend school and university, and to participate in fields traditionally denied them.

This is important work but access alone is insufficient. Permitting women a public voice to use language and literary forms historically denied them means little if they must comply with perspectives, language rules, conventions, and protocols which devalue or ignore or misrepresent women. We become, as Gail Scott noted, "little men" or end up, as Helene Cixous once warned, "doing men's writing for them."

The grammar and lexicon of language is also seen as problematic for women, and has been a more difficult issue to address than women's silence in the public domain. This is evident in the ongoing debates concerning gender-sensitive or politically correct language. The most obvious indication of sexism in the language lies in the semantic denial or degradation of women. Using "he" or "man" as a referent to all of humanity is the classic example. This seemingly innocuous convention reinforces the notion of woman as absent and therefore, when she is present, particularly in nontraditional locations (e.g., the boardroom or website) she can be more easily viewed as aberrant (Spender, 1980; Lakoff, 1975). Historical research indicates that words, titles, and metaphorical language with originally positive terms referring to women and female kinship (e.g., spinster, hag, dame) have become pejorative in far greater numbers than comparable terms referring to men (Schulz, 1991).

But sexism in language goes beyond words and phrases. It has been suggested that the very forms and styles of sanctioned writing and speaking favor, or are more suited to a male-centered reading of the world. The formal essay, for example, is often cited as a distinctly masculine form of writing, but even the sentence has been called into question. Virginia Woolf, at one point commented that she considered the sentence too heavy, too pompous for a woman's use (Woolf, 1984). It has been suggested that traditional narrative structure with its single authoritative storyteller, well-motivated characters, single crucial conflict deterring the protagonist from some ultimate goal, and the quick movement to closure reflects patriarchal mastery in Western culture. Such a structure, whether the product of social relations or of an inherent psychosexual history, is often considered inadequate by some for representing women's experience (Friedman and Fuchs, 1989).

Operating from a revisioned psychoanalytic framework, French feminists Cixous, Irigarary, and others have called for women to "write the body," that is, to write and celebrate women's difference, and in doing so, to create feminine writing forms, styles, metaphors, and lexicon to reflect the rhythms of women's bodies and of their experiences more generally. This has meant forms that break with linear time, logic, and closure, and a move towards more fluid forms and styles.

On another level, Deborah Cameron (1998) provides a particularly vivid example of how discursive practice fails the interests of women. She quotes two newspaper reports of rape. One from the *Daily Telegraph* [London] reads, " A man who suffered head injuries when attacked by two men who broke into his home in Beckenham, Kent, early yesterday, was pinned down on the bed by intruders who took it in turns to rape his wife." The other from *The Sun* [London], reads " A terrified 19-stone husband was forced to lie next to his wife as two men raped her yesterday" (p. 11). The act of rape is presented in both these reports as a crime experienced by the husband. It is the husband's feelings that are described, and it is the husband who is the grammatical subject of the verbs "forced" and "attacked" and even "suffered."

Considering how women's language use has been and continues to be channeled, considering the sexism inherent in the grammar, structure, and form of language, and in light of discursive practices that frame and produce meaning, it is not surprising that feminists have come to describe language as "man-made," as the "oppressors' language," even as a "foreign language." Women writers must contort or challenge dominant discursive practices in order to represent their experience from a perspective outside of gendered power relations. All women face this task to some extent, but for women writers who choose to write deliberately, conspicuously, and subversively as women, a category intersected by class, race, ethnicity, and sexual orientation, the task is formidable. It means breaking with an identity of woman as a nonparticipant within the public domain, or as a "little man" or a "cross-dresser" mimicking androcentric discursive practices. It even may mean breaking with an identity of women as white, heterosexual, and middle class. This is not only a practical problem for women writers, it is also a crucial political struggle for feminists in their efforts to expose and dismantle the interlocking gender, race, and class oppressions and privileges in discursive practice and to find new ways of speaking and writing the world—to create new and radical identities.

The "Tradition" of Feminist Avant-Garde Writing

As part of their craft, male and female writers have always sought to bend and rework language and literary form to suit their purposes. However, to write of themselves and their experience outside of dominant discourses, writers must radically contort language and literary practices in order to break from the meanings and subject positions structured by those practices. Feminist literary scholars have done much to recover work of women writers who have challenged traditional language and literary practice. Until recently much of their scholarship focused on the writings of white Anglo-Saxon women in the nineteenth and twentieth centuries. From this history, limited as it is, it is possible to identify various contortions women have made or have been forced to make in order to write of themselves outside dominant discursive practices. One obvious contortions was to write anonymously or using a male pseudonym. Jane Austen, Mary Ann Evans (George Eliot), Aurore Dudevant (George Sand), the Bronte sisters, among others, resorted to this tactic largely in order to secure publication.

Some women writers use subplots, minor characters, and patterns of imagery to subvert dominant values and assumptions operating in conventional story lines made available within the genre. Gilbert and Gubar demonstrate in the work of Jane Austen the duplicity of the happy endings of her novels, "in which she brings her couples to the brink of bliss in such haste. . . or with such sarcasm that the entire message seems undercut" (1984, p. 169). If we accept Gilbert and Gubar's assessment, it is possible to see Jane Austen as attempting to subvert the dominant story line in romance genre that posits marriage as the only possible ending, and marriage and motherhood as the ultimate satisfaction for women.

Radical and more blatant efforts to subvert rather than simply to contort language and literary form are evident in the work of Virginia Woolf, Gertrude Stein, Dorothy Richardson, Djuna Barnes, Jean Rhys, and Anais Nin, among others. The work of these women provides a rich but largely ignored tradition of women's experimental fiction, which is only now being recognized as worthy of consideration separate from the work of male experimental writers, and of particular importance for feminist literary scholarship. The work appears very contemporary despite the fact that much of it was produced in the first half of the century. Gertrude Stein's exploded syntax, Djuna Barnes' flat dehumanized characterizations, Dorothy Richardson's stream-of-consciousness writing, and the blurring of genres by Anais Nin predate by decades similar kinds of experimentation now occurring in feminist writing communities. These early women were already engaging in the linguistic and literary sabotage suggested by Luce Irigarary in her call for women to write outside of patriarchal discourse "by overthrowing its syntax—by suspending its eternal teleological order, by snipping the wires, cutting the current, breaking the circuits, switching the connections, by modifying continuity, alternation, frequency, intensity" (1971, p. 36). These women usually worked independently and did not form networks with other women writers, much less declare a social movement. Anderson and Zinsser (1988) have suggested that these women writers became "honorary men" in the eyes of their male and female contemporaries, and were often shunned rather than supported. Yet as "honorary men," these particular women were creating what would later be called *"l'ecriture feminine"*—a feminist writing practice.

In recent years women writers have experimented with language and literary practices with a sense of freedom and boldness that no previous generation of women has ever known. Spurred on by the energy of the women's movement of the 1960s and 1970s, supported by academic work in women's studies and linguistic theory, nurtured by feminist presses and journals and by grassroots political activity, women writers as a group have subverted a wide range of literary and language practices. Wendy Waring (1987) has catalogued the kinds of literary experiments published in Canada by feminist journals such as *Fireweed, Room of One's Own, (f.)Lip,* and in general literary periodicals such as *Contemporary Verse,* and to some extent in feminist academic journals such as *Canadian Women's Studies* or *Resources for Feminist Research.* As Waring indicates, much of the work in the 1980s and 1990s has focused on innovation at the level of sound and representation of sound. The most common experiments erase and/ or replaced male referents: e.g., wommin, womin, or womyn. Quebec feminist writers have often altered the grammatical gender of French. Nicole Brossard for example, entitles a section in her novel *Lovhers* "Ma Continent," changing the noun continent from masculine to feminine. Mary Daly in her classic text *Gyn/Ecology,* transgressed many traditional spellings and created new words that reconstructed meanings to suit her purposes as a feminist. She created words like ILegiti-Mates, Crone-ography, Fore-Spinsters.

In some of the most difficult and certainly disruptive feminist linguistic experimentation, meaning almost becomes secondary as the reader and author explore how language supports the social order. Audrey Thomas creates a disjointed text through spelling and syntax, as evident in this small sample of her writing:

> cild child. My child was killed. My child was chilled. In my womb, the child-hama, the child curled like a shrimp or a sea-horse and clung to the slippery decks.
>
> (in Tregebov, 1987, p. 18)

Erin Moure toys with language by chaining categories of words together in a section of her poetry:

> knife is a verb
> bayonet is a verb
> coat is a verb
> she knife, she coat,
> absolute the bayonet
>
>   (in Tregebov, 1987, p. 20)

A number of feminist writers also experiment with the format of their work on the page. Marlene Nourbese Philip, for example, in her poem "Discourses of Language" has sections that read along the outside margins of the page. Writers have also reworked the role of reader, author, and subject, often blurring these three categories. In her work "The Women in This Poem," Bronwen Wallace turned her female reader into a character in the poem. With this step, Wallace broke with the traditional male omniscient author-narrator, and created a connection on the basis of gender between reader, writer, and character. Other efforts have been directed toward reclaiming the female body from inscription within patriarchal discourse. A number of writers have experimented with alternative images and word rhythms that emulate the body. In several of her works Nicole Brossard has attempted to rewrite the maternal body, giving it a more positive sensual quality than it has been traditionally accorded. Of course, these are not the only kinds of language and literary experiments taking place within the community of feminist writers, but they are indicative of the kind of work that has been and continues to be attempted by feminist avant-garde writers.

Horizons of Meaning

In light of the problem of women and language, feminist avant-garde literature would seem to offer a large reservoir of practical strategies and techniques for women to draw on in articulating their experience. More importantly, these practices form part of a distinct tradition or literary formation that offers alternative readings of the world and of the self, and so alternative possibilities for identity and identifications. With particular reference to poststructural notions of identity, Teresa de Lauretis writes:

> Different forms of consciousness are grounded in one's personal history;
> but that history—one's identity—is interpreted or reconstructed by
> each of us within the horizon of meanings and knowledges available
> in the culture at given historical moments, a horizon that also includes
> modes of political commitment and struggle. Self and identity, in other
> words, are always grasped and understood within particular discursive
> configurations. (1986, p. 6)

Discursive configurations or boundaries entail much more than
rhetorical strategies and techniques, but include shared assumptions,
unstated premises, and interpretations that delineate a set of possible
meanings, or what de Lauretis calls a "horizon of meaning."

Feminist avant-garde writing defines or configures an alternative
"horizon of meaning" that includes an alternative conception of the
female subject. Perhaps the most systematic and detailed articulation
of the horizons configured by feminist avant-garde literature is
evident in the journals that publish this kind of work. While acknowledging that other sites, e.g., conferences, personal networks, books,
and newsletters, also serve to collectively define the tradition, I suggest
that the journals, in order to be accountable to their readership, are
forced to state overtly the current and most important premises and
practices by which they operate. By doing so the editorial staffs of
these journals collectively concretize and stabilize, to some extent,
their genre, delineating its most obvious boundaries.

In English Canada, feminist avant-garde writing is configured in
journals such as *Fireweed, Room of One's Own, Tessera* and the now
defunct *(f.)Lip*. The pre-publication brochure for *Room of One's
Own* and the opening statement in the first issue of *(f.)Lip* capture
some of the primary tenets of this kind of writing. The brochure for
Room of One's Own reads:

> "Culture" as we know it is Male Culture and if women's stories are to
> be properly told, new forms of expression and format are needed. As
> women work at developing these forms, they need access to publication
> in order to share their ideas and build their own sense of competence.
> (reprinted in 1977, vol. 3 (1), p. 76)

Ten years later, the opening editorial of the first issue of *(f.)Lip* reads:

> There already exists an exciting body of work by feminists who basic-
> ally write in traditional narrative and lyric forms. We are proud of these
> texts. In our experience, publication and dialogue space is being firmly
> established for this work. There are grey areas, blurred boundaries, of
> course, but (f.)Lip aims to publish the work of women writers who
> are attempting to write outside or sometimes, more accurately,
> alongside this tradition. . . . To state it simply, we are interested in
> new work which explores and alters content, form and language in ways
> that disturb our normal reading patterns, ways that delight, startle,
> subvert and liberate. Ideally we are looking for work which will
> inscribe us as women in a new literature.
>
> (March, 1987, vol. 1 (1), p. 1)

It is evident that feminist avant-garde writing carves out a space exclusively for the development of a women's culture. This assumes that cultural practices are not politically neutral enterprises, but are produced within relations of power. Because of gendered relations of power, women have been excluded or marginalized such that what is deemed "culture" is in fact "male culture." By suggesting that women's culture(s) had not existed outside of its designation and representation within patriarchal culture(s), both journals invoked a monolithic notion of patriarchal power, and gestured towards an essentialized notion of "woman" awaiting inscription in literature.

According to the editorial statements, this inscription and the development of woman's culture, demanded competency in speaking outside of patriarchal discourse. Such a competency requires two conditions: 1) a separate cultural sphere exclusively for women; and 2) new language and literary practices. Innovative feminist writing has been produced exclusively for and by women so that the practice of the journals and presses is to publish female writers who explicitly and conspicuously write for a female audience as part of a com-munity of women writers, readers, editors, and publishers. It is assumed that this community consists of those who identify them-selves through a collective identity as women, and see themselves as sharing a common history of gender oppression, and so see the political necessity of a women-only space. This is stated directly in a 1991 *Fireweed* editorial:

We imagine Fireweed's audience of women includes or could include every woman who looks to the writing of other women for sustenance, who accepts that there are concrete reasons for women-only designed space for sharing our creative and theorizing work.

(*Fireweed*, 1991, p. 5)

This separate space allows for interaction between and among women that encourages or sustains the building of women's culture(s) and alternative visions of oneself and the world. It is a culture built through acts of reading and writing in which writer and reader refers to woman writer and reader, even to the point that the designation "women" disappears or almost disappears as it does in dominant literary traditions in which the writer is assumed to be male. Note the description of writer in *(f.)Lip*: " Women. Feminists. Mothers. Daughters. Writers (i.e., women writers of any class, race, religion or sexual preference)" (May, 1988, p. 1). The woman writer is not aberrant, and does not need to be marked within this tradition, as she is in male dominated canons. She is a writer, not a "woman" writer, although evidently the parenthetical information is still necessary. The creation of normality supports the struggle against the practices and identities offered in dominant discourses.

The need evident in the parenthetical information to further define the "woman" writer, and by extension women's culture, to include differences of class, race, religion, and sexual orientation among women speaks to difficulties in what is often assumed by th notion of woman. The editors of *(f.)Lip* speak specifically to the both the desire and the reality of the tradition:

(f.)Lip is a great big net, a web that weaves its way forever outwards trying to support and communicate between all women—Women of Colour, white women, Lesbians—a network that works for all women if you will. This web also serves as a safety net; a place where women are encouraged to express themselves in innovative ways. . . . The web has not fulfilled its function. Though white women have struggled to make a place for themselves in the publishing world. Women of Colour continue to go unseen, unheard—unpublished. What we have instead of a web is a ladder—the white woman's ladder . . . In contrast to a ladder, the strength of a web comes from the outer edges; the foundation is on the fringe. And it is the fringe that we at (f.)Lip must continue to listen to.   (September, 1989, Vol. 3 (2), pp. 1–2)

The assumption of whiteness within the category of "woman," as well as other assumptions about class, ethnicity, etc., must be considered as part of what has defined feminism and feminist avant-garde writing, at least until recently.[2]

In addition to creating a separate culture exclusively for women, the second condition for the development of a women's culture, according to the journal statements, is language and literary experimentation. As stated in *Room of One's Own:* "if women's stories are to be properly told, new forms of expression and format are needed"—a new literature: a "mother tongue" is required. The statements of the journals indicate that feminist avant-garde writing defines its energies not only against male culture specifically, the male literary tradition, but also against, or alongside women's writing, or feminist writing that lies within conventional language and literary practices. Although creating a space for women writers and readers remains important, it is paramount that what is published subvert conventional language practices in the name of feminism, with the intent of creating an alternative—creating a new home for women in language:

> Many writers, certainly most feminist writers, have had to leave their homes in some essential way, and that's a lot of what writing is about. It's like writing home, not back to the home you came from, but writing your way towards a home you're making for yourself and for others.
>
> (Warland in Williamson, 1990, p. 308)

The third aspect of feminist writing described in the journals concerns specific kinds of reading and writing pleasures. The work should operate "in ways that disturb our normal reading patterns, ways that delight, startle, subvert and liberate." The text should startle the reader. Some have suggested that all avant-garde poetry is disruptive and that that is part of its charm, part of the pleasure it affords. Roland Barthes makes an interesting and important distinction between traditional and avant-garde texts in terms of the emotions they elicit. The former, he suggests, offers pleasure; the latter, bliss. Barthes writes:

Text of pleasure: the text that contents, fills, grants euphoria: the text that comes from culture and does not break with it, is linked to a comfortable practice of reading. Text of bliss: the text that imposes a state of loss, the text that discomforts (perhaps to the point of a certain boredom), unsettles the reader's historical, cultural, psychological assumptions, the consistency of his [sic] tastes, values, memories, brings to a crisis his [sic] relation with language.   (1975, p. 14)

This suggests that the emotional experience of reading feminist avant-garde writing can be quite different from that of more traditional texts, offering, at least initially, bliss rather than pleasure; that is, the loss of self rather than the confirmation of self and the world. This loss, in particular, involves losing an identity of "woman" produced in patriarchal culture, opening up the possibility of redefining oneself within feminist discourse(s).

The sense of self recreated within feminist discourse(s) is not fixed or stable. As Gail Scott comments, feminist writing

cuts across taboos not only of dominant ideology, but also those that arise as our feminist awareness attempts to structure new "meaning" for women. For me, consciousness [is] . . . inevitably accompanied in writing by the temptation to transgress these very limits of vision through the play of language. (1989, p. 116)

Because of this continual pushing at the structures, the home and the subject positions created in language are constantly under renovation, constantly shifting and changing. Current innovation in feminist writing can be seen only as a springboard to further experimentation with language and literary form and the further naming and renaming of the self and the world. This constant flux prevents a hard and fast prescription for feminist writing and for a feminist vision(s) of the world. The sense of self and the world created in this tradition is only and always provisional.

With this kind of literature, then, the reader and writer expect and delight in the texts that startle and subvert conventions in ways deemed meaningful to a feminist project. The reading and writing are acts of exploring and potentially destroying and rebuilding one's home in language. Exploring, destroying, and rebuilding requires risk-taking: crossing from what is known to what is unknown or perhaps even unknowable; from the safety of the familiar to the unfamiliar in which the possibility always exists, even remotely, that what may be found might be unpleasant, dangerous, or troubling. The writer or reader contends with such a possibility and with the certain knowledge/desire that she may be forever changed in the process. But she looks forward to the prospect:

> I think that the feminist reader who is drawn to experimental writing wants to be challenged, wants to see the radical impact feminist consciousness has had on our writing and thinking, and wants her presence as a reader to be changed as a result.
>
> (Warland in Williamson, 1993, p. 304)

Such work is not easy to read or create. Di Brandt describes the difficulty and the joy of leaving her strict Mennonite community to become a writer who participates in acts of linguistic sabotage demanded in this genre:

> It was hard to leave that country, that clean land. Hard to find a way into the impure, no longer so clearly centred, confusing modern world. Hard to find words for this wild journey. Hard to become a writer, committing perjury all the time against the sacred Book. Letting the wildness into the words. Transgressing, remembering the old fear. Listening to the earth and the women, breathless with desire, wanting so much the dance and the laughter, the unholy babble of speech.
>
> (Brandt, (f.)Lip, 1988, vol. 2 (1), p. 20)

The pleasure in reading and writing within the literary formation of feminist avant-garde writing—of "letting the wildness into the words"—lies in the fears and joys of self-reconstitution. The fear comes in transgressing the comfortable and familiar, and the fact that one is working with language does not make the act any easier. Heather Prince comments that being a woman writer means

> learning to ride something dangerous (pick what you will) and not being afraid. It's a lot of not being afraid. Now what could be safer than words? —bears, perhaps. Perhaps.
>
> ((f.)Lip, 1987, vol. 1 (3), p. 11)

The Female Subject in Feminist Avant-Garde Writing

The principles, practices, and pleasures that configure avant-garde feminist writing in Canada, at least within the feminist literary journals of the 1990s, can be summarized by the female subject produced within their "horizon of meaning." It follows from the description given in this chapter that the subject position "woman" made available within this writing formation redefines femininity. Personified, she is an active, radical, writer/reader who uses language and literary practices to explore, produce, and subvert the world and her identity in that world. She sees gender as a central category and gender oppression as a common unifying experience of all women. Reading and writing are seen as powerful social and political acts in the building of women's culture and in the redefinition of "woman" outside the referent of man—outside the notion of "Man's Other," literally to become "womyn" or "wommin." For this woman, creativity means breaking with literary and language forms and practices in new and meaningful ways, as opposed to working within convention. It is expected that creative reading and writing acts will be personally and socially disruptive, but this unsettling is viewed as a positive and productive experience. It is part of the pleasure of reading and writing. She is a writer/reader who finds pleasure in actively exploring and subverting language forms and practices and who views all discursive constructions as open to continuous redefinition through language and literary experimentation. Feminist avant-garde writing would seem to produce a woman who, within the frame of feminism, writes publicly, subversively, and creatively to order to reconstitute herself as "woman" in the world. It would seem a very powerful construct for women readers and writers.

An Education in Reading: Riding Something Dangerous

Feminist avant-garde writing in Canada is not well known outside of literary circles and occasional university classes. For most women education in reading and writing has been quite different from that provided by feminist avant-garde writing. The criticism often levelled at this work is that it is difficult, dense, and inaccessible to most readers. Nichole Brossard in an interview with Janice Williamson, has argued that this difficulty arises from a lack of experience:

Janice: In making these new textual spaces for the reader's pleasure, how do you deal with criticism about inaccessibility or elitism?
Nichole: When you read a book you have the choice of whether to take it or leave it. If you take it, you have to be willing to do some work on your own part as a reader. You also have to develop a habit of reading. With experience you can read "difficult" books more easily. Through le nouveau roman and postmodernism there has been a kind of education in reading. The more you are able to follow what the writer has been doing with language, the more you enjoy your reading, because you also are playing and recreating the game which gives you pleasure. (Williamson, 1993, p. 69)

The education in reading offered in schools is far more familiar, if less powerful. It is not surprising that other discursive forms appear strange and difficult, but this does not have to remain so. My study explored an alternative education in reading for young women in secondary schools, examining the potential of feminist avant-garde literature and its practices, premises, and pleasures. It focuses specifically on how a group of six young women negotiate with the subject of "woman" produced in this literature, and on the affective and intellectual investments that underpin their negotiations with and against "her." The theoretical framing, as well as the details concerning the research methodology, pedagogy, and specific literature deployed in the study, are the focus of the next chapter.

Chapter Two

The Scene of Writing and Research

Like many a feminist critic before and after me, what I most wanted to do at first was set up a Women Writers course. Such a course resembles Charlotte Perkins Gilman's utopian Herland—a feminist enclave at the edge of the patriarchal academic empire, a utopia probably without male colleagues and possibly even without male students, where only texts by women are discussed and by a kind of critical parthenogenesis women without the aid of men produce analyses of the writings of women.

—Alison Easton, 1989

My research involved six high school girls enrolled in a creative writing class. These students were asked to respond to a selection of feminist avant-garde writing, orally, and in creative and expository (journal) writing. As outlined in the introductory chapter, the intention was to determine the nature of the intellectual and emotional investments that sanction particular subject positions, socially, and that may secure identification psychologically. The focus on writing, in particular on creative writing, was not accidental. The act of composition can be an intensely intellectual and emotional activity, in which identities are made and broken. This chapter sets the scene of the writing and research in the study, by theorizing writing as an act of identity formation, and further delineating the nature of identification. On a less abstract note, it also describes, briefly, the material context in which the study was undertaken—the scene of the writing and research.

Writing as Performance: Identity as Performative

Judith Butler (1997, 1993, 1990) posits all identities, including gender, as performative; that is, as a stylized repetition of acts, gestures, and movements through time that creates a recognizable self. For Butler, it is not that the performative *expresses* an essentialized identity existing prior to enactment, but rather that the repetition of acts *constitutes* identity. The acts, gestures, and postures have a history that creates the illusion of an inherent, stable self, but the illusion can be exposed. Butler writes,"what is called gender identity is a performative accomplishment compelled by social sanction and taboo. In its very character as performative resides the possibility of contesting its reified status" (1997, p. 402).

Writing can be seen as a kind of stylized act or practice through which identity is constituted. George Otte (1995), for example, refers to writing as performance or "invoicing": what in a more general sense, Jane Gallop (1995) refers to as "im-personation." From a poststructural perspective, Pam Gilbert suggests that "writing is about taking up a particular speaking position in a discourse and then bringing certain subject positions into existence" (1992, p. 194). To write is to produce a subject position and in this performance to create or produce other subject positions. Writing can be a risky enterprise, particularly when working in the genre of the avant-garde, since it means deliberately disturbing the more familiar performative acts of identity in one's reading and writing practices. Disturbing the act stops, if only momentarily, the easy repetition and reproduction of the self. In doing so, avant-garde writers, consciously or not, expose the illusion of an essentialized self, and offer the possibility of other identities against those that have been deemed natural and normal. Further, there is the indelible evidence of the author's subversion of identity—the print on the page. Feminist writers display their failure to conform to traditional performances of femininity in reading and writing practices. Not only do they fail to be silent in the public sphere but, adding to their transgression, fail to write 'in pink' respectfully and appropriately.

Such audacious writing may be exciting but it is also unsettling, both to read and to produce, as Betsy Warland (1993) so candidly admits,

Writing can be dangerous. When you are expected to belong in a home that is acceptable, socially or politically or religiously, but you don't, and you write beyond it—it can be very dangerous. . . In *Serpent (W)rite* [her book] the risk was literally feeling that I was going to lose myself, my direction, everything, that I'd go off the edge of the page, the world. (in Williamson, 1993, p. 308)

There is risk but there is also potential reward. Luce Irigaray (1971) suggests that women have alternative desires screaming to be spoken, but unutterable in the present symbolic order. Experimental or avant-garde writing that demands the reworking of conventional literary acts allows one to say the unsayable, to recreate the world and recreate a self. Anais Nin writes

I believe one writes because one has to create a world in which one can live. I could not live in any of the worlds offered to me. . . . I had to create a world of my own, like a climate, a country, an atmosphere in which I could breathe. (1967, p. x)

The possibility for reconstituting the self is enticing and all the more possible in writing because the act in and of itself can be destabilizing. Gayatri Spivak argues that the "scene of writing," that is, the composing process, requires absence as its necessary condition. The "sovereign authorial presence" does not exist in the writing process. Spivak notes that "when a man [sic] writes, he is in a structure that needs his absence as its necessary condition (writing is defined as that which can necessarily be read in the writer's absence)" (in Crowley, 1989, p. 34). Sharon Crowley explains Spivak's comment: "That is, when (if) a writer writes he does so because the desired audience isn't immediately present. Its 'presence' is fictional. It 'exists' only insofar as the writer imaginatively embodies it, as some construct of future readers" (1989, p. 34). The immediate absence of the audience and the eventual absence of the author requires the writer's pluralization. The writer must become both author and audience to her work. At the very least, she must imagine the audience and their reactions, knowing that without her presence, the audience will create her intentions, desires, and meanings. That is, at the time of reading, the author of the text is absent and thus is fictionalized by the audience. These absences and pluralizations make writing a complex and potentially destablizing process. These characteristics, along with the possibility that alternative repressed or suppressed desires are screaming to be spoken or produced, suggests that writing may be an ideal vehicle for individual and social transformation: a place to let wildness into one's words, into one's life. As Helene Cixous observes "writing is precisely the very possibility of change, the space that can serve as a springboard for subversive thought, the precursory movement of a transformation of social and cultural structures" (1980, p. 249).

This is obviously a very different idea of composition from what is usually posited in English/Language Arts classrooms. For example, in schools deploying a classical model of education, writing is used primarily to domesticate or discipline individuals to the reified forms and codes of society (de Castell, Luke, and Egan, 1986; Morgan, 1987). Writing, through rigid adherence to form, is viewed as a tool to stabilize and refine individuals and society by exposing all social classes to particular norms and practices of literacy deemed by those with power to do so as inherently worthwhile or valuable. Conformity is key in this model. In schools where a social progressive orientation dominates, writing is viewed as a means of discovering one's self and one's world. Creative writing is particularly important since it is seen as a way of safely naming and sorting through the tensions and problems of everyday life. Thus, writing is, in essence, a form of therapy organized through a process of self-discovery and self-examination (Dewey, 1938; Brand, 1980; Morton and Zavarzadeh, 1991). In this model writing serves to remedy instability, rendering an individual coherent, and integrated.

Here, against both classical and progressive models, I claim quite the opposite—that the writing process itself can be destabilizing, but therein lies its promise for emancipatory pedagogical work. In this view attention and value shifts from developing social conformity and self-coherence to some of the qualities of postmodernity: to what is partial, incomplete, reversed, altered, missing, or excessive, with the intention of exploring, not remedying, what is aberrant. In part the aim of this study was to look for and explore moments in which the constitution of a familiar, conventional identity was disturbed in acts of reading and writing the feminist avant-garde.

The Research

Methodologically, this study drew on the growing research tradition of critical ethnography and on feminist approaches to ethnography and interpretative research. Critical ethnography investigates the complex dialectical relationship between social structures and human agency. It assumes that individuals are not passively reproduced by social structures and practices but actively produce themselves with and against ideological and material forces. It is a research paradigm that developed from increasing dissatisfaction both with "social accounts of 'structures' like class, patriarchy, and racism in which real human actors never appear" and with, "cultural accounts of human actors in which broad structural constraints like class, patriarchy and racism never appear" (Anderson, 1989, p. 249).

Critical ethnography takes as a given that research, researchers and subjects are located within political/historical contexts that determine institutional and personal histories. This means that there exists no objective or unbiased space in the process of knowledge production. Research is always "interested," necessitating intense reflexivity and self-critique in any research design. The overriding goal of critical ethnography is social transformation, and so it is not surprising that the tradition merges with neo-Marxist and feminist theory (Anderson, 1989). Feminist researchers who work within critical ethnography see gender as a central category, albeit interlocked with other forms of difference (i.e., race, class, sexual orientation) that mediates the conditions of women's lives. Critical feminist ethnographic research generates its problematic from women's experiences and perspectives in ways relevant to ending women's inequality. It is work that serves the interests of women; it is research *for* women. There is often an emphasis on lived experience and the significance of everyday life and on how individual women make meaning of their experience. The research designs often attempt to break down the hierarchical relationship between researcher and researched.[1] There is a concern with "producing emancipatory knowledge and empowering the researched" (Lather, 1991, p. 70).

Although my study did create a strong "dialectically educative encounter between researcher and researched,"as Patty Lather suggests, largely because it involved a teaching situation, the actual intent

was to expose students to the literature, not necessarily to empower individual students with the research findings per se. The students did
not participate in the analysis of the data, nor did I attempt to break
down the relationship between researcher and researched (the students). In this study the fact that I was both teacher and researcher
confounded my attempts to break down this relationship since both
positions, teacher and researcher, have tremendous institutional power.
However, my study fits loosely within the category of critical
ethnography and more specifically within critical feminist research. It
was, for example, work committed to social transformation, namely, to
improve women's lives by seeking to understand the discursive
formation of gendered identity. It was work focused on improving
school literacy practices and feminist pedagogy for the benefit of
young women. It looked at young women's negotiation with and
against the subject positions organized within literary formations. It
was work that at times disrupted the conditions of its telling in order
to maintain a level of self-criticism and reflexivity particularly
concerning issues of representation. Finally, although this research
was not an extended ethnographic study of the lives of young women,
traditional ethnographic methods and materials often employed in
educational settings were used; that is, interviews, field notes, student
writing, and classroom talk.

Data for this study consisted of descriptive evidence of students'
emotional and intellectual responses to the literary materials, both to
the published works and to their own work as presented and discussed
in the seminar classes. Data was collected from taped audio record-
ings of each seminar and interview, from samples of students' creative
writing, and from written comments in journals kept by students
during the study. The classroom talk, journal writing, and creative
writing offered three places where students could respond to the
practices, premises, and pleasures organized in the feminist literature
read in the seminar classes. The classroom discussion and journal
entries allowed students to discuss their responses to the literature, and
the creative writing allowed students to work with or against the
practices and premises evident in the feminist writing in their own
writing.

From this material the data collected consisted of specific
moments when students experienced the premises, practices, and pleasures of feminist avant-garde writing as the same as their own, and
moments when they marked the practices as different, odd, and/or

unacceptable. Instances of similitude were identified as those when students expressed their agreement with the premises of the literature, when they imitated or adopted the practices and premises as their own in their writing and speaking, when they expressed their pleasure with the poetry, and when they expressed their similarity to (or desire to be similar to) a character or to a subject position offered in the writing. In other words, significant moments were those when students seemed to overtly identify with the female subject organized in feminist avant-garde writing and instances when they clearly did not. Also important were moments of struggle with the literature and with the study, expressed as hesitation, uncertainty, confusion, and/or irritation when they experienced "trouble with text" (Bennett, 1990).

The naming of this data is based on the premise that identity is organized through a play of similitude and difference. In other words, the boundaries of identity are formed by whom or what is seen to be like and unlike ourselves. To use a very simplistic example: to "be a girl" is to see other girls as generally similar to oneself and boys as generally different. From the perspective of poststructural theory to see oneself as a girl requires that one participate within those sets of discourses that name girls as similar and boys as different. If identity is performative, as Judith Butler posits, it is to perform in ways that constitute similarity to girls and difference to boys in acts, gestures, postures, etc. Disrupting the play of similitude and difference can prompt a renegotiation or reconstitution of self. This may occur with exposure to any unfamiliar material and discursive forms and practices. It can also prompt intellectual confusion and emotional upset when the new material cannot be easily incorporated as like or unlike one's self. This should not be surprising. Education of any kind can be said to disturb, upset or interfere with what is known and what is familiar (Britzman, 1998).

As stated earlier in this chapter, the play of similitude and difference that structures identity is organized through identification (who we want to be) and desire (whom we want to have). Identification is the process of incorporating the "other" into our selves, and the "other's" desires as our own. Thus desire and identification instantiate identity, as Diana Fuss suggests, "Every identity is actually an identification come to light" or a series of identifications (1995, p. 2). Identity is the public remnant or effect of one's social and psychic history of identification. In this study I looked to moments of identification in which there seemed overt evidence of incorporation of, or refusal of and/or distress with feminist avant-garde writing, examining instances that seemed highly charged as possible indications of a volatile history of identification. Attention here was not primarily on the participants' personal histories and circumstances of identification, but the focus was on the general history of adolescent girls and their loss of connection with their parents, their difficulty with positioning in Western culture, and their more complex relationship to language. Data was analyzed in terms of this social and psychological context.

It should be noted that identification is a psychological process not yet well understood by theorists. What is generally agreed upon is that identifications, produced at least in part in the unconscious, are mobile, elastic, and volatile, open to sway of fantasy and difficult to predict (Fuss, 1995). As such, they may be well beyond one's own control, much less the control of a feminist teacher; nonetheless, understanding what is at stake for young women in their acceptance or rejection of feminist possibilities is an important step if some attempt at pedagogical intervention is to be undertaken. Examining the responses of young women to feminist avant-garde literature for evidence of struggle over identity and traces of identification offered one path of investigation.

The Study, the Students, the School

The participants in this study were grade twelve students enrolled in a creative writing class offered in a large, co-educational, multi-racial, multiethnic secondary school located in a suburban neighborhood in a large urban center. The creative writing class was not part of the core program but an elective class that students chose out of a number of courses to fill out their program. All the students expressed interest in reading and/or writing; four of the six young women in the study wrote creatively as a hobby, five of the six read for pleasure, and all expressed enthusiasm for reading.

The six students were all seventeen years old at the time of the study. Rebecca, Denise, Janet, and Lauren are Caucasian, Zandra is South Asian, and Thea is of Asian ancestry. The school was located in a middle-class neighborhood, and so I suspect the girls were middle class, but I cannot confirm this. Neither can I absolutely confirm their sexual orientation. What I can say in regard to sexual orientation is that all of the students spoke or wrote during the project about boys and boyfriends in a way that suggested they were claiming hetero-sexual identity. Like many high schools in the area, the student body was highly diverse, both racially and ethnically. Students indicated that there was little racial or ethnic tension in the school. The school administration and teaching staff seemed to be sensitive to or at least aware of issues of race and gender. During the time of the study a series of events was being planned for Black History Month, a special seminar was organized for grade nine and ten girls to encourage their enrolment in math and science courses, and numerous students and teachers participated in the "White Ribbon Campaign," a program designed to increase awareness of issues concerning violence against women. According to the students in my study, there were teachers on staff who self-identified as feminists. Women writers were featured prominently in their English literature curriculum. Furthermore, I experienced no difficulty in securing school or school board approval to conduct my research, which I presented as a study focused on female students and their response to innovative feminist writing.

I gained access to the students through a teacher who was teaching a creative writing class. The teacher, Mr. C., was, in my estimation, a very charismatic teacher, although I am certain he would deny this. The students in the study spoke of him often and with an odd blend of affection and irritation. From my formal discussions and casual observations, it appeared that Mr. C. framed his creative writing pedagogy largely from a psychological model informed by the theories of Progressivism. This was most apparent during my initial visit to his class:

> Mr. C. had the students create ink blots of sorts using ink and folded paper. The students place a blob of ink in the fold line of a piece of white paper. Folding the paper and placing pressure on the ink and then unfolding the paper created an abstract shape. The students were to make several of these and then, choosing one that inspired them, that "spoke to them," write a poem on the page with the ink blot. Using creative writing as a vehicle to tap at the subconscious or at the emo-tional life of the students seemed to be at the heart of Mr. C's understanding of creative writing. (My Research Journal, November 6)

The perspective and the literature that I would offer the young women in the study would be quite different from that which they had experienced with their creative writing teacher.

Mr. C. solicited volunteers from the class for my study as well as making private appeals. The students he chose to speak to privately were students he believed had a genuine interest in writing and were in his estimation "good" students, that is, students who would be enthusiastic about the study, which he entitled "The Women's Writing Project." Eight students volunteered, two of whom would drop out early in the study because of scheduling difficulties. Six remained in the study.

The students met as a group during class time once or twice a week for approximately three months. There were interruptions in the schedule due to school holidays and examination weeks. In total the group met twelve times. I directed the sessions. During the sessions the literature selected was read and discussed, the girls' own work was read and discussed, and/or students worked individually on journal entries or on their creative writing pieces, written in response to the selections. The work in this study replaced what they would have been doing in their creative writing class. None of their work was graded. At the end of the study the students were interviewed individually. They were asked about their response to the project as a whole and about their poetry and journal entries. They were given a copy of the transcripts from their interviews and given an extended opportunity to elaborate, clarify, alter, or comment on what was in the transcripts or on any other aspect of the study.

The young women read eighteen literary works during the course of the study. The specific titles are listed in the appendix. The selections included works by contemporary French, Anglo, Asian, Black, and Native Canadians published in the 1980s or 1990s in issues of three Canadian journals: *Fireweed, (f.)Lip,* and *Contemporary Verse.* All of the works were written by women for women and offered a wide range of unconventional uses of language and literary form. Some works blended traditional forms of poetry and prose; some of the poems had strong visual components; some transgressed rules of orthography and syntax and/or semantics; some displayed unconventional arrangements of line and verse. Several featured multiple narrators or "voices." Themes studied in the literature included mother-daughter relationships, sisterhood, female childhood, female friendship, women's immigration experiences, alcohol and substance abuse, homelessness, and urban violence. A few of the selections were celebratory in tone, but the majority offered quite harsh and depressing depictions of life. (Oddly enough the students indicated that they preferred such depictions.) Although there was one work of fantasy, in general the writing might be categorized as expressive realism.

The literary works reflected my predetermined assumptions about the interests and abilities of high school girls and the institutional constraints of time and place. Since the study was conducted within the context of public school, the school board, parents, and the creative writing teacher needed to approve the materials. Works chosen had to conform to their standards and were selected with that caveat in mind. Because there is only limited time during the semester and during class, short prose and poetry made up the teaching unit. It seemed important to allow students to experience a range of contemporary feminist writing rather than to focus intensely on a limited number of works. Although some of the literature was preselected, alternative literature was presented to reflect the interests and abilities of the six students. For example, a number of poems concerning sisters and female friendships were introduced into the study when the students indicated their enthusiasm for these topics. A few poems were made available for individual reading. These poems are also included in the appendix. At times the students shared their own writing in the seminar. Occasionally students brought in poems that they had written for other classes or poems that they had read outside of school and wished to share.

Pedagogically, I envisioned the seminar classes to be much like Easton's class described at the beginning of this chapter—a feminist and female enclave at the edge of patriarchal secondary school forms and practices. My desire to organize such a place and to see the students as the "objects of my emancipatory desires" obviously affected the pedagogy (Lather, 1991, p. 141). As it turned out the class was much like Easton's in that it was a space exclusive to women for the discussion of women's writing. I also wanted to expose students to feminist avant-garde writing, a literary formation in which I take much pleasure. I was investigating students' identification with this literature from the perspective of someone who has identified with it. The echoes of my surprise and dismay at the unfavorable responses to some of the selections that reverberate in the data chapters are a result of my own affective and intellectual investment in particular literary formations and more generally in a feminist emancipatory project. This was not an easy study for the students or for me.

The pedagogical approach to the literature taken in the seminar classes drew on reader-response methods and perspectives. Sessions began with a discussion of personal responses to the content and form of the literature and then extended to broader social concerns related to these responses. In these latter discussions it was my intention to ensure that first and foremost gender remain at least one focus of the conversation and in doing so that commonalities among women as well as differences be emphasized. I also wanted to ensure that the form of the writing, in particular the innovation or experimentation attempted, was highlighted in our discussions. The general assignment or "invitation" of the study was to engage in feminist avant-garde writing in one's own creative or journal writing, either in terms of form or content. In other words students were offered an opportunity to work with the premises, practices, and pleasures of feminist avant-garde writing—to embrace or dance with the "woman" constituted in the literature. Individual and collective responses to this invitation are described in the next four chapters.

Chapter Three:
Threatening the Good Writer

Rebecca

I think that you should know that I'm not a feminist. I believe that
almost all men are scum and that every woman should have every right,
but I don't follow or have any wish to follow all of the feminist issues.
— From Rebecca's second journal entry

At the time of the study Rebecca was a seventeen-year-old grade
twelve student, who was enrolled in a creative writing option class.
Rebecca is Caucasian and I suspect middle-class. She described herself as an avid reader and writer. In addition to working on school
assignments, she wrote creatively in her spare time as a hobby and was
at the time considering a career in journalism. Rebecca mentioned her
love of reading several times and indicated a preference for mysteries,
science fiction, fantasy, historical fiction, and the classics. Despite the
heavy demands of her course work, including her creative writing
class, Rebecca produced a great deal of written material for the study,
more than any of the other students. Although initially admitting
she "didn't really like writing journals," Rebecca wrote over fourteen
pages of single-spaced, handwritten entries, and eight poems that
totalled 155 lines. In her journal entries she responded regularly,
thoughtfully, and in great detail to the materials and issues raised
during the study.

This is not to say that Rebecca always found pleasure in the
poetry read and discussed, or that she simply and unproblematically
identified with the principles, pleasures, and practices of feminist
avant-garde literature and the identity of "woman" it constructs.
Indeed, what is particularly interesting about Rebecca is how intensely
she interacted with the literary materials, and yet how tenaciously she
negotiated against what this writing would seem to offer. Rebecca
largely refused the female subject position organized in the feminist
literature, but refusal was not easy. Although Rebecca described her

experience in the research study favorably: "It was basically positive," there were many moments when she expressed strong dissatisfaction, uncertainty, confusion, and even anger. Rebecca's intense negotiation with the feminist literature of the study was informed by
particular notions of reading and writing pleasure, and by traditional
concepts of "good" literature.

Reading and Writing Pleasures: Escape and Rescue

Rebecca, like a number of the other students in the study, wrote
frequently in her journal and spoke often in class about her own
writing. In her first entry, dated November 11th, she began, "I don't
really like writing journals, so I'll make this short. I really enjoy
writing. When I write I can escape from this world and enter into
another." Although in this initial entry Rebecca wrote only three
paragraphs, every entry that followed was more extended. She seemed
to enjoy discussing writing in a context that supported her interest.
Evident in the first few lines of the entry are the pleasure and
purposes of writing for Rebecca. The theme of escape permeated
much of what she said about her reading and writing practices during
the study. Throughout her journal she referred to writing as a plea-
surable form of escape. In her second journal entry she wrote, "When
I write, I try to escape from my problems and worries or the usual
boring things, which occupy my life." In one of her poems, Rebecca
described her imagination as "deep, dark and secretive," as a place
of "happiness," and as "a world that is wrapped tight around me like
a cloak."

Like writing, reading was also described as a form of escape and
entertainment. Rebecca admitted she likes to be "swept away" by her
reading, at one point commenting, "I like a book that you can get lost
in. The best books make you forget about almost everything around
you." She listed her favorite fictional characters as Sherlock Holmes,
Robin Hood, King Arthur, Doctor Who, and James Bond. Idealized,
legendary, and romantic male figures, it is not surprising that the
story she was currently writing in her spare time was patterned after
the Robin Hood story. When asked about why she wrote stories set in
the past, Rebecca wrote, "I like to write about things from the past,
because to me, the past always seems better than the present or
future."

Rebecca did change her views slightly later in the study when I asked her directly if she must escape to a better place. She stated, "The world in the book doesn't necessarily have to be better. I like different worlds. They're much more interesting and exciting." In her journal she described her writing as significant recreation in her life: "It's sort of like a hobby. A very important hobby." But whether Rebecca entered a different and exciting future or a romantic past in her writing, she did not place herself as a character overtly in such settings. As she stated flatly, "I find I can't write about myself or other people I know personally, and truly escape into that other world and enjoy it."

The pleasure Rebecca experienced in her reading and writing hobby was evident throughout the research project. There was an exuberance in her tone when she wrote in her journal that she, "really, really enjoys writing"; she found she could "truly escape" when she could "write freely." At one point, she described writing as superior to reading: "Reading is almost as exciting as writing." But of course, she was referring to a specific form of writing: autobiographical writing did not create the same pleasure; nor did school-based writing assignments, which Rebecca described as too restrictive in terms of content and too anxiety-producing because of deadlines and grades.

As outlined in Chapter One, feminist writing is understood as a social and political act. This is quite different from the notion of writing as a pleasant and innocuous escape from life's problems. Historically, the notion of writing as a personal hobby has been commonly associated with women since they could not assume or had difficulty assuming a public voice. Indeed personal or hobby writing was viewed as an entire appropriate pursuit for literate, genteel women. The distinction between writing as a hobby and writing as a serious political act serves to differentiate a traditional feminine pursuit from a radical feminist act. At this point Rebecca did not make a distinction between feminine and feminist writing but instead separated reading and writing for school from the reading and writing she did at home as a hobby. The pleasure of escape that Rebecca experienced in her writing is obviously attached, at least in part, to the lack of teacher surveillance. As a hobby Rebecca had greater control over her own purposes and pleasures for reading and writing.

Valerie Walkerdine (1990) has suggested another reason for the value placed on writing as a hobby and a form of escape. Walkerdine posits that fantasy offers a vehicle for the relatively safe exploration of difficult conflicts and uncomfortable emotions. The more fantastic the content, the better the engagement, and the greater the value to the reader. Although there is no actual escape, the difficult problems and emotions do exist, but can be safely explored in symbolic form in the different and fictionalised worlds created in the text. Walkerdine writes,"the positions and relations created in the text both relate to existing social and psychic struggle and provide a fantasy vehicle which inserts the reader into the text" (1990, p. 85). Pleasures, problems, and conflicts can be safely explored in writing fantasy or escape literature, but evidently such escape was not available to Rebecca in feminist literature. Rebecca made such a comment during the interview:

> Helen: This is different from what you would normally write?
> Rebecca: Yes. Well, I was trying to use the forms of the poems you gave me so I was trying not to, like, copy them but to use the same kind of writing and then maybe a slightly different theme so I couldn't really escape because I was using a certain form.

With reading and writing pleasures organized in terms of writing as a hobby in which the reader/writer can escape from problems and boredom of everyday life, Rebecca struggled with the literary material and practices offered in the class seminars. She struggled between writing as a personal escape, and writing as an overtly social and political act, set in the all-too-real present. She struggled between her notion of the writer/reader who escapes into fantasy to cope with the problems and/or boredom of life, and the writer/reader in feminist avant-garde literature who confronts the problems of life, and more specifically, the politics of women's lives through fantasy or fiction. Rebecca's struggle was evident in her strong efforts to establish and reestablish her writing pleasures and perceptions in the face of the feminist writing offered in the research project. Initially, for example, she stated and reiterated in her journal and class talk the pleasures and joys in writing as escape. As the study continued, the distinction Rebecca created between feminist writing and her own writing played itself out in the conflicted style and content of the creative writing she produced and in her discussion of the poems. However, she did attempt to adopt some of the practices evident in the feminist literature studied in the seminars.

The first set of poems Rebecca submitted seemed to reflect an intense effort to work with the literature. The first poem was quite personal, set in the present, and described "The Mundane Trials of Life," presumably trials in her own life. The few lines of this poem read:

> i am sick and tired of the mundane trials of life
> the need to think the need to react to what is
> placed in front of me i want to get away but
> i am trapped beneath the glass forced to struggle
> and fight against it i do not see the purpose
> of certain things they do not seem clear
> they are clouded like the stranger lost in the fog
> why do people follow the paths that were set
> why don't they make new paths new hopes new
> dreams for themselves . . .

Rebecca ended her poem in capital letters, "SOMETIMES I NEED TO GET AWAY FROM THE MUNDANE TRIALS OF LIFE." The other two poems she submitted together with "The Mundane Trials of Life" were sections from a Robin Hood story she had previously written and then reworked for the study. The first she entitled "Sections from 'Baltzavar' (a Robin Hood Story)" began, "a strong wind blew around them and leaves blew in their faces they could hear nothing but the wind . . . baltzavar fingered the blood red pendant . . . squeezed it tightly letting its magic flow around her she breathed deeply." Her second effort, "Parts of 'the Minstrel's Family' (a Robin Hood story)," read "we feel great pity and sorrow for his poor wife she must sit by her window day by day waiting for a chance to escape from her ruthless husband and the cage he has put her in . . . perhaps she will fall in love and her true love will rescue her from the sheriff's sharp talons and set her free."

In terms of form, Rebecca attempted in all three poems to use what in the seminar classes was referred to as block style: a form with no punctuation or capital letters that was characteristic of Angela Hrynuik's poem "the hairdresser," one of the first poems read in the study. In content, the stark, personal declarations of Rebecca's first poem are in obvious contrast with the more romantic descriptive narratives of the last two. In class Rebecca commented that the attempt to rewrite her Robin Hood poetry "did not work" in her opinion, and for the duration of the study she did not return to previously written pieces or attempt a romantic fantasy.

The first set of poems are similar in theme. The theme or the problem of entrapment—a need to "get away from the mundane trials of life" and of the "poor wife" who must "sit by her window day by day waiting for escape"—is obvious. In the Robin Hood excerpts escapes were accomplished through magic and a rescue from a "true love" who will "set her free" rather than through direct action by the female protagonists. This contrasts with the content of the poems in the study, in particular, "I Fight Back," a poem written by Lillian Allen that Rebecca indicated she liked very much. A section of Allen's poem reads, "I FIGHT BACK/ Like my Sisters Before Me/ I FIGHT BACK." Although this poem also contains a notion of escape or rescue, it describes an individual woman taking action in a long history of black women: "sisters" who fought back rather than wait for rescue. Identification with women who fight back can be considered a form of rescue, but Rebecca did not entertain this possibility in her poems.

Desire would seem to play a role in this. For young women claiming a heterosexual identity, escaping with women might not have the appeal of waiting for a male lover-rescuer. In waiting for a male rescuer, female passivity becomes connected to pleasure and desire. Rebecca's Robin Hood stories and poems create a male rescuer who, because of his true and perfect love, will rescue the female protagonist from her problems. She must only "sit by her window" and wait. This is a common narrative line. Valerie Walkerdine notes that girls' comics, among other forms of literature for girls, often "prepare for and proffer a 'happy-ever-after' situation in which the finding of the prince (the knight in shining armour, Mr. Right) comes to seem like a solution to a set of overwhelming desires and problems" (1990, p. 88).

Lillian Allen's poem "I Fight Back" breaks the narrative line connecting femininity, passivity and heterosexuality, as do the other poems in the study and, I would argue, as does feminist avant-garde literature in general. Within the context of feminist avant-garde writing produced at the time of the study, the male lover-rescuer is unavailable, almost unutterable. At the point Rebecca wrote "I believe that almost all men are scum," she too seemed less than enamored by the real men she had encountered in her life, but she continued to retain a belief in the fictional male characters who populated her reading and writing. In fact, her strong belief that almost all men are "scum" may have fed into her desire for the ideal male characters she found in the fiction she read.

Rebecca liked the poem "I Fight Back" for the strength of the main character, but she did not take up the possibility of women rescuers. Race may also have played a role here since identification with Black women may not have offered Rebecca a viable possibility. But it may be that Rebecca's difficulty with the practices and pleasures of feminist avant-garde writing rested more in the working out of heterosexual desire and passivity.

Rebecca did not return to writing romantic fantasies during the study. Although she did not elaborate on why her efforts to rewrite romantic fantasies using the stylistic formats evident in the feminist avant-garde selections "didn't work," I suspect it had to do with the inability to explore the connections between desire, passivity, and heterosexuality. If "escape" is organized, to some degree, through this connection, it would seem impossible to operate within the genre of feminist avant-garde writing as it was configured in the selection of poems offered and available at the time of the study. The fact that Rebecca was willing to attempt to put away romantic fantasy may indicate how important her identity as a writer—as someone who is interested in exploring writing—may be to her.

Marking (or Not) Gender and Race

While the male lover-rescuer may not have been available in this study, female friendships and maternal family relationships certainly were. Following a session in which the students read and discussed Bronwen Wallace's poem "Between Words (For Carole)": a poem written for and about the author's friend Carole, all the students chose to write about female friendship. At no other time was there such a convergence of interest among the young women in the study. Their energy and enthusiasm, as indicated by the amount of work generated by this one poem, may signal a moment of identification in which the young women in the study could negotiate their writing and their sense of themselves easily within the boundaries of feminist avant-garde writing.

Rebecca chose to write a very celebratory poem about her friend Zandra. The poem speaks of Zandra's buoyancy, strength, kindness, and humor, and ends with an urgent call, "No matter what happens in the world, Don't ever, ever change." There was pleasure in the writing of this poem. Rebecca wrote in her journal that she was in a "good mood" when she wrote about Zandra—that it was "fun."

Zandra is a South-Asian Canadian and yet in Rebecca's poem there is nothing that would suggest that Zandra's ethnic or racial background is different from Rebecca's, with the exception of Zandra's actual name which has been changed in the text here. Although there is nothing conclusive in the data, I wonder whether Rebecca might see Zandra as more likely to change because of her racial and ethnic heritage, particular in the context of a Canadian society that makes her "other." Although in class Zandra did not name or adopt a more definitive South Asian-Canadian identity, in the future she might and that together with time, might alter and disrupt their friendship. No doubt Rebecca likes Zandra, but considering racial and ethnic difference, it is interesting that Rebecca would implore Zandra to remain the same; perhaps remaining the same means not highlighting difference.

Of course, it is not only racial and ethnic differences that may have been suppressed. There is nothing in the poem to indicate that Zandra is female. While the explicit marking of gender (and, increasingly race) is a dominant feature of feminist avant-garde writing, Rebecca does not constitute Zandra within these markings. So that while the feminist literature allowed Rebecca a space to write about female friendships, an opportunity she took up with great enthusiasm, she refused to specify or highlight "femaleness." Rebecca simply refused the explicit marking of gender and race offered in the feminist literature. In the context of poetry read in the seminars, the poem on Zandra served to reestablish or stabilize a female identity, largely unmarked by gender and race. Rebecca's refusal to explicitly mark gender and race is evident in the numerous poems she wrote about herself with one odd and interesting exception.

Although Rebecca initially indicated at the outset of the research study that she did not find pleasure in writing autobiographically, she ended up writing six poems about her own life. She wrote with great energy but did so in a manner quite different from the feminist literature. Although Rebecca attempted to use the feminist poems selected for class, the identity Rebecca produced in the majority of her poems was generally a self completely detached from the political and social world, without social markers, much like her depiction of Zandra.

This was particularly evident in a poem she submitted, entitled "The Inner Debate." A section of it reads as follows: (The slash lines are part of the work.)

> I feel lost sometimes/sometimes/a lot/ You think you're alone/ I am alone/ purposely/I don't know, I don't think so . . . /You can't relate to people can you/they can't relate to me/ it's a two way street/ it's a one way street with a dead end . . . /Is there any hope for you/ Maybe/Why/There's usually some hope to be found somewhere.

Without social markers or context, the subject of the poem is knowable only to the writer. The poem is thus quite personal and very private. This poem is in direct opposition to the practices and premises of feminist avant-garde writing in which the writer, reader, and subject of the poem are explicitly identified as female, sometimes in concert with other designations (race, class, etc.), and where writing is viewed as a public and political endeavor rather than as private, personal exploration. Finding it impossible to draw on her usual premises and pleasures in writing, yet wanting to write about her life, Rebecca turned to an alternative conception of creative writing rather than work within the practices and politics of feminist avant-garde writing. Her move to a personal and psychologically marked self is evident in a selection of Rebecca's journal in which she writes about the technique she used in her poem "The Inner Debate":

> The writing technique (the back and forth response) helped me express my feelings in a better way than prose would have. I released some of my anger and frustration when I wrote this. It was kinda beneficial. . . . I find that I write more powerful poetry when I'm depressed and angry.

Rebecca told me that she wrote the poems "The Inner Debate" and "The Mundane Trials of Life" when she was feeling very depressed. Writing at this point was framed not only as a means to escape from difficult problems and emotions, but as a process that itself offered escape through the therapeutic exploration and release of strong emotions. In doing so, Rebecca drew on the psychological discourses that, as outlined in the Introduction, have structured the purposes and importance of creative writing in school curricula since the 1930s. As described in Chapter Three, this discourse was strongly articulated in the practices in operation in Rebecca's creative writing class, so she was quite familiar with the discourse.

I also want to point to the multivoiced writing that characterized Rebecca's poem and several of the feminist avant-garde poems, selected and read in the seminars. These kinds of poems were favorites of Rebecca's and a number of the other students as well. Read through the psychological discourse on creative writing, it may be argued that multivoiced writing permits the release of tensions, ambivalences, and contradictions that might then allow the reunification of the personality, and the reestablishment of a coherent identity. Within this frame the maintenance of multiple and contradictory selves or voices is regarded as pathological. However, in postmodern theory identity is viewed as never stable, or coherent, but dynamic and fragmented. Multivoiced poetry simply displays the common and everyday circumstances of many contradictory subject positions vying for, and experienced by, the individual.

As described in Chapter Two, the category of "woman" is always or ideally in flux in feminist avant-garde literature. The instability of identity thus is a concept that seems to overlap both the psychological and postmodern/feminist discourses on writing. In this instance, the overlap allowed Rebecca to represent her experience using a literary technique taken from the feminist poems but read through a psychological and therapeutic discourse of creative writing. By negotiating it this way, she could neatly avoid the social politics of feminist writing and the possibility of identification with the "woman" created within in its parameters.

The failure to mark herself and Zandra, and the invocation of the psychological and therapeutic discourses on creative writing suggest Rebecca's strong desire to avoid the gender and race differences that are so central in feminist avant-garde writing. The question is what affective and intellectual investments or commitments underlie this desire. The explanation may be simple. The psychological discourses concerning creative writing are sanctioned within school curriculum while feminist discourse vis-a-vis avant-garde writing are marginal at best. It may be that Rebecca drew on the discourses with which she was most familiar: those which she has been most strongly educated in and rewarded for as a "successful" student. It may also be that Rebecca sees herself as a promising writer and would like to produce what traditionally has been deemed "good" literature.

Signs of "Good" Literature

Rebecca's commitment to traditional notions of literature influenced her negotiation with and against the feminist writing. This became evident when she expressed her dissatisfaction and confusion with Carla Murray's poem "I saw a Monster."

> It didn't really seem like a poem. It was like she [the author] just picked a bunch of pictures and then typed the words out. But I don't know, I guess, I'm just more conservative . . . . It did seem like she kind of threw it together. It almost seems as though she had taken someone else's work and just written something over it. She's like, manipulating their words. I don't like it and I do like it. It's creative but I don't know if I can really think of it as a poem.

Writing that follows particular rules, that demonstrates a reverence for language, was, or at least had been for Rebecca, the hallmark of literature. She did try to write outside language conventions in the first set of poems she submitted, but it proved difficult, and she wrote later in response to her attempts, "Stories need punctuation and proper grammar. Stories should be able to pass something like a certain fact to their readers. Poems can get away with being abstract. I don't know why." In her next entry, her definitions began to unravel and her confusion was obvious. She wrote:

> When I said that stories have to get some sort of fact across, I was probably wrong in some ways. It's just that most stories have to have a set of characters, plot, and setting. Poems are like forms of art (not that stories aren't). They can be looked at and admired for the meanings different people gain from them. . . . Stories can have hidden meanings but not so much that a reader can't comprehend the plot. Forget it! I've lost myself now. I don't even know what I'm trying to say.

Irreverence to and subversion of traditional literary form and language convention is, of course, the very hallmark of avant-garde literature. This was disturbing for Rebecca, and she attempted to reaffirm a more traditional notion of literature and the necessity of rules and conventions. Her investment in more traditional literary form and content may lie in her identity as writer. Rebecca spoke in the journal entry previously cited as having lost herself and, while in this instance she was referring to her argument, metaphorically she was in fact losing a sense of herself in working with the feminist literature. Her identity as a successful writer who works within literary convention was placed in jeopardy by deploying feminist avant-garde practices. In the study, Rebecca had to become (or perform) a "woman" writer who breaks the rules, which is quite different from how she defined herself as writer. In her journal she repeatedly described herself as working within convention, showing deliber- ateness and thoughtfulness in her writing. At one point, Rebecca commented that in the earliest stories she had written, the "writing style seems simpler. I hardly put any detail in them. I also didn't put too much thought into what I wrote. I just rushed through things without planning them."

But while planning required thinking, literary and language con- ventions did not. Rebecca noted how conscious she had to be when using unconventional forms. In her journal she wrote: "Last session I tried to write a piece of prose writing using the method from 'the hairdresser' where no punctuation or capitalization was used. I found it kind of hard because I had an irresistible temptation to add periods and commas." Normally, "I don't usually have to think about it."

Suppressing the "irresistible temptation," that is, struggling with literary form and content, was not what Rebecca liked about writing; instead the writing should come almost "without thinking." She commented during the interview:

> I liked writing this one [pointing to one of her own poems] and that one, and I'm not sure. The other ones were more forced. . . . It was nice because I hate it when you have to sit there and think, like, what am I going to write. I just wrote it without thinking. The pen went by itself almost.

Rebecca's ability or desire to write so comfortably, so effortlessly, within convention that she need not think about form and content, gestures to the traditional notion of the writer: an individual with natural talent who effortlessly works the conventions of literary form and style. But I suspect there was something more at play here. Feminist avant-garde writing provides an alternative identity—the woman writer who breaks literary convention—which requires a self-consciousness about language, form, and content that prevents the author from being "swept away" by the writing process, if indeed that ever happens. In the quotation previously cited, Rebecca indicated that she "just wrote it [her poem] without thinking. The pen went by itself almost." The pen went by itself: the writing just happened. The "pen" controlled the writing. Indeed there was little for the writer to do but allow one's self to be overcome by strong emotions—to be swept away by the experience. Her description of writing and her pleasure in writing hearken back to Romantic notions of the inspired writer under the control of his/her muse, and to the view of writing as an emotional experience and a therapeutic and deeply personal enterprise.

Rebecca did not entertain easily or willingly the notion that literature can be overtly political or politically motivated, and, in general, she did not accept the specific politics that informed the feminist literature in the study. This was apparent in her interview as she struggled to explain why she didn't like one of the poems in the study, 'I Saw a Monster': "It seemed like for Women's Liberation or something. It's something you might see on the wall and the graffiti and all that. . . . Well, I guess some poems—poems don't seem like they should be political. I don't know why."

Although there was hesitation in her voice, Rebecca was reiterating the discomfort she felt with feminism and more generally with writing as a political act. She considered the work to be radical and several times during the study named herself explicitly as conservative. It was of some surprise, considering what she said, that Rebecca indicated an interest in avant-garde films. When I asked about this contradiction, she replied, "I don't know, maybe conservative is safer, like, when you're writing. The books I'm reading, I try to, well, I don't really read poetry books that have modern writing in it. I like historical fiction but they are basically conservative." Rebecca's frank concern with safety speaks to the personal and institutional risks in reading and writing exercises. If, according to Rebecca, these risks are absent in viewing avant-garde film, then feminism may lie at the heart of her discomfort. In the context of this study what is the nature of the personal and institutional risks of feminism.

There were two instances when Rebecca directly refused feminism and the marking of gender. At one point Rebecca listed her favorite fictional characters. In reading her list I was dismayed by the fact she did not include even one female character, and somewhat horrified by the inclusion of James Bond, a character I consider to be the best (worst) example of male machismo. In efforts to keep gender at the fore, I wrote in the margins of her journal, "no female characters?" The question, together with the poetry read that day, triggered a response in her next entry. After a paragraph describing her writing as a form of escape, Rebecca followed with this:

> The fact that most of the characters who [sic] I like are men, is something which I really never thought about before. I didn't like sit down and decide to admire an all male set of characters. It just sort of happened.

Rebecca never did tell me of any female characters she liked. Her journal statement reiterated her refusal to specify or mark gender difference, in this case with fictional characters. Rebecca did not elaborate on why fictional characters were her favorites. Looking at her list that included Sherlock Holmes, Robin Hood, King Arthur, Doctor Who, James Bond—it is apparent that the characters are intelligent, intrepid romantic figures. It is possible that Rebecca can more easily identify with these characters and with their personal qualities if their gender is not an issue. Moreover, the heroic qualities of these characters and the fantasy that surrounds them may be threatened if considered in relation to feminism and feminist literature. It is difficult to know, but Rebecca did make a connection between feminism and the denigration of men later in the same journal entry. After writing about the innovations she employed in her own writing, Rebecca abruptly switched topics to speak about feminism:

> I found that writing traditionally was much easier than writing radically. I think that you should know that I'm not a feminist. I believe that almost all men are scum and that every woman should have every right, but I don't follow or have any wish to follow all of the feminist issues.

For Rebecca feminism evidently signalled a belief that "all" men are "scum," and if all men are reprehensible, so, too perhaps, are Rebecca's favorite characters. But, if a distinction can be maintained between actual men who are "scum," and male fictional characters who are favorites, then a deep desire or longing for the ideal man, even though he can only be found in story, is also maintained.

Feminine heterosexual desire may fuel reading and reading pleasure. For the young women in this study, both reading and desire may be threatened by the feminist literature.

But, the distinction here between male characters and living men, and the refusal to name gender difference in fictional characters previously cited indicates an even more complex and difficult reading position that Rebecca and the other young women in this study may have been attempting to secure. By not explicitly designating the gender of characters, the female reader can identify with male characters and their qualities. By carefully separating real men from fictional characters the female reader can long for ideal men in her fictional characters. She can both *be* them and long for them. This is a tenuous position for heterosexual women because if a female reader identifies too strongly with a male character whose object of desire is a woman, then the female reads women as objects of desire, and a homosexual or bisexual reading position is produced. If the female reader desires the ideal man who, as rescuer, must possess an active, aggressive, and intelligent nature, then marking those qualities too strongly as "male" prevents the female reader from identifying with those qualities. Divesting male fictional characters of their explicit gender marking would seem important in helping to produce a reading position for women that secures identification with qualities not usually available in the rigid binary of masculinity and femininity. Feminist avant-garde literature and its explicit marking of gender violently disrupts this identification, as well as the organization of a heterosexual reading position.

The refusal to specify gender is evident in terms of character but also in terms of the reader and writer. At one point in the interview I asked Rebecca what she found most positive about the project. She replied: "I like to know what other people in Canada are writing, and I like the idea of just experimenting with the form and knowing that there are other forms you can use. I learned things like that." Despite the fact the project was explicitly and deliberately focused on women poets and women's experience, Rebecca refused to name, yet once more, that it was women writers she had studied. Instead, she used the nongendered term "people." Of course it is quite possible that she may have been interested in "what other people in Canada are writing," but evidently she would not highlight women in that interest.

Marking Student/Marking Gender

Towards the end of the study the "I" that Rebecca had produced in her writing shifted suddenly from the unmarked, psychological "self" to one specifically organized and named as "student." In her writing and classroom discussion Rebecca spoke several times about the unequal power relations between teacher and student. Her frustration and anger found expression in her poem "Dear Teacher." In her journal she described the poem as "slightly abusive" because she was angry at one of her teachers.[1] She explained that because of her anger "for that teacher, I felt anger for some of my other teachers, and the poem became a sort of hate note towards any teacher in general." Rebecca did not volunteer any specific information about the incident that triggered the poem. However, there was some indication in the poem itself. A section reads:

> Everything is ordered, commanded and barked
> Everything is ordered, commanded and barked
> You're always right; I'm always wrong
> You're always right; I'm always wrong
> You're always right; I'm always wrong
>
> I can't stand you for that, dear teacher.

In this poem students are defined by their lack of power, subject to the capricious orders and commands of their teacher. Using the theme of oppression made available in the feminist literature, Rebecca wrote from this position but not as a female student. By naming or marking herself as "student," she apparently did not risk femininity or heterosexual desire. However, in the last poem she took the risk.

In her last poem Rebecca again focused on students and teachers, but this one time she marked gender. The poem, entitled "My Film Arts Class," described a class of unruly students and an uncaring, incompetent teacher. Both the unruly students and the uncaring teacher were marked as male. It began:

> The teacher told the class to be quiet and so,
> their voices grew louder
> The teacher talked of Orson Wells, Mise-en scene, and montage
> and so,

they mocked him with heavy sarcasm
The teacher was too lazy to write the lesson upon the board,
and so
He focused the camera on himself and dictated
We were forced to see a movie we didn't like
and so,
They threw popcorn and made lewd comments
with a vengeance

The "we" is distinct from the "they" who threw popcorn and made lewd comments. In the final lines of her poem Rebecca identified the "they," and finished with what I would describe as a feminist comment:

My Film Arts is comprised almost completely of boys
They say that women are illogical and so in comparison
What does that say about my film arts class?

In this poem, as in "Dear Teacher," Rebecca adopted the subject position "student," as part of the "we" being "forced" by the teacher, but then she differentiated male students. Although she did not mark herself as a female student, she did so indirectly by explicitly naming "boys." In the last line Rebecca aligned herself not simply with female students but with women in general. The alliance was formed on the basis of common oppression, specifically the stereotyped representation of women as illogical creatures. Perhaps the connection was also forged on the basis of the boys' "lewdness," that is, sexual and possibly sexist comments, unchecked by the male teacher, that aligned Rebecca with women generally as the objects or subjects of such comments.

Despite the distance she created between herself and feminism, for this one time Rebecca broke with the sanction against gender politics, and seemed to identify, momentarily at least, with the subject position offered in feminist literature. The question is why was it suddenly possible for her to do so. Why was it suddenly possible for Rebecca to write outside traditional notions of good literature by marking gender and acknowledging women (including herself) as oppressed? In part it may be that the gender dynamics in the film class were so intense, so personal, and obvious, they were impossible to ignore. Perhaps the writing in the study provided a means for Rebecca to understand and

name her experience, and the study, a venue to express quite justi-
fiable anger. It is also possible that the tenets of feminist writing were
becoming more familiar, and Rebecca, who described herself as a
good student with a strong interest in writing, was simply adjusting to
the premises, practices, and identities available and valorized in
feminist writing. However, what might well have made this shift
possible was a particular production of heterosexual desire that was
inadvertently supported in the feminist writing. Rebecca's last two
poems depicted teachers and male students as reprehensible. Rebecca
was clearly disgusted by them not as individuals but as a group, but
there was no risk in admitting this; indeed such admissions may have
fuelled her longing for the ideal man found in literature. Feminist
literature in which men are named directly or indirectly as a problem
allows for Rebecca's description of the young men in her film arts
class. Although the literature of the study did not make available the
possibility of pleasure in symbolic men, Rebecca could, at least
engage the literature in its apparent anti-male sentiment. Thus, it was
possible for Rebecca to move in the last lines of her poem to the
feminist statement that women are unfairly named: "They say that
women are illogical."

Rebecca took a stronger feminist position in this poem than she
did at any other time in the study. Even at the end of the study,
during the interview, she refused the position. I asked her whether she
was bothered by the exclusive focus on women writers in the study.
She replied, "I think its important to talk about this, but I think they
sort of went on and on about that one subject, like no one went out
and wrote anything different. It's just how women are treated like
scum and that was about it." However, Rebecca did say, "I don't
know. I think that some poems should be written like this [feminist]
but I think these poets could write more like on different subjects.
There are other subjects. It just seems that all the poetry coming out
from women in Canada is like on how badly we are being treated but
there is nothing else."

It was surprising that she suddenly positioned and identified
herself as gendered, using the term "we." But generally, it was not a
position that she seemed to feel comfortable with or would easily
acknowledge. Later in the interview I asked Rebecca about whether
her film class poem had improved:

Yeah. (She laughs). Almost my whole class is boys. There is a couple of girls but they skip a lot so there basically is only three girls in the class. And the other two are hardly there. And I don't know if I was being manipulated or not but I felt as though I was being ignored. No one really listened to me. The first term we had to do a film and, I don't know, I went to a group and asked if they needed any female actresses 'cause they were short of those and they couldn't think of anything to write so then it sort of got into an argument between the group. One guy was really into it and the other people weren't. And we were talking about ideas for scripts so then someone said I should write a script and I wrote it and someone else wanted to write one and they didn't actually get around to doing it so then they said since I wrote the script, you might as well be the director so I was trying to run this film but people won't show up and things like that and they were really acting immaturely like they fool around and we never got the film finished.

Although she reiterated the gender composition of the class: "Almost my whole class is boys,"—she suddenly used generic, nongendered terms—"people," "they," and "anyone." Although clearly the "people" acting immaturely, and "fooling around" were boys, and, although she claimed the importance of this fact in her poem, she would not refer to gender in our interview. By avoiding gender, Rebecca avoided the feminist subject position. It may be that while she could identify with the unjust treatment of women, she did not want to lose the possibility of the ideal male and the desire organized in more traditional discourses on writing and literature. Of course she was only seventeen and this was a relatively brief albeit intense encounter with feminist literature.

Feminist avant-garde literature offered Rebecca practices, premises, and textual pleasures that were, I suspect, quite different from those that she had been exposed to previously. Her understanding of creative writing, good literature, and reading and writing pleasures that she described initially in the class seminars and rearticulated in various ways throughout the study, spoke to psychological and classical discourses about creative writing and the identity of writer/reader that have dominated English studies over the last hundred years (Brand, 1980; O'Neill, 1992). Rebecca's insistence on writing as escape, as a hobby, and as a medium for personal, private explorations of a psychological "self," in which language and gender consciousness is a distraction, and that "literature" is or should be defined as work produced within conventional language or literary practices indicated that she formed her identity as a writer largely in opposition to feminist literature.

Rebecca worked with energy and intensity during the study. She made what I think of as heroic efforts to work with the literature as best she could in light of her strong investments in more traditional discourses and in terms of a particular form of heterosexual desire. I suspect her sense of herself as "good student" and as a "good writer" may have kept her in the study. She was able to engage with feminist literature by largely disregarding the gender and racial politics that supported the readings of the works studied. Although Rebecca responded to feminism by distancing herself from a feminist identity, she did use a feminist analysis in at least one of the poems she wrote. The conditions of the study opened up an avenue for her to write autobiographically, producing a social identity as woman and as student. Although she declared herself conservative, she attempted in her creative writing to break with conventional writing practices. Rebecca's negotiations with feminist avant-garde literature were complex. She did not embrace the "woman" constituted in feminist avant-garde writing, but she could walk with her (and me) in writing about the injustice she experienced as a student and, finally, as a "female" student.

Two Samples of Rebecca's Poems

My Film Arts Class

The teacher told the class to be quiet and so,
their voices grew louder

The teacher talked of the film he saw last week
and so,
they yelled out what they knew and thought
about it.

The teacher talked of Orson Welles, mise-en
scene, and montage
and so,
they mocked him with heavy sarcasm.

The teacher was too lazy to write the lesson
upon the board
and so,
He focused a camera upon himself and dictated.

We were forced to go see a movie we didn't like
and so,
They threw popcorn and made lewd comments
with a vengence.

My Film Arts is comprised almost completely of
boys,
they say that women are illogical
and so,
in comparison, what does that say about my
Film Arts class?

Dear Teacher

I despise you like nothing I've known.
Deep within me a burning ember of fury is growing.
Deep within me a burning ember of fury is growing.
You haunt me with your cursed looks.
You haunt me with your cursed looks.
You haunt me with your cursed looks.
Memorizing, repeating, paraphrasing and enacting.
Everything is ordered, commanded and barked,
Everything is ordered, commanded and barked.
You're always right; I'm always wrong
You're always right; I'm always wrong
You're always right; I'm always wrong.

I can't stand you for that, dear teacher.

Chapter Four

Threatening the Good Student

Thea

In this world
we are constantly surrounded by others
unable to escape them
and yet,
utterly and unbearably
alone.
You do not know me.

—from Thea's poem "Looking Deeper"

At the time of the study, Thea was a seventeen-year-old grade twelve student. She is Asian-Canadian. Her parents immigrated to Canada prior to Thea's birth. Thea was in the same creative writing class as Rebecca but, although acquainted with each other, they were not friends. In the first session Thea introduced herself as a "good student" and then, fearing she sounded "conceited," later explained in her journal "I meant good, not only in English but all my classes, in the sense that I do my homework every night and pull off good enough marks, like, I don't have a problem with whatever my teachers assign." She continued, "I didn't mean good in the sense that I get awesome marks, etc. To be honest, English is probably my worst subject. I am a Math person." For Thea, a good student, as she would describe to me, is someone who complies with the demands of of teachers regardless of interest or abilities in the subject area. Although there may be specific cultural elements at play I was and am unaware of, including my own preconceptions, I suspect this identity, one shared by a number of the students in the study, is related to the image or construct of the "good girl" as polite, compliant, and concerned for the welfare of others. The images of the "good girl" and the "good student" evoked by Thea and Rebecca and the other students in the study were not unique. The subject position of "good girl" "good student" and for that matter "bad girl" or "rebel" are produced with some variation across a number of discursive fields. Among others, Valerie Walkerdine (1990), Carol Gilligan (1990), and Michelle Fine & Pat Macpherson (1992) have described the qualities that comprise these identities: conformity, compliance, moderation, and control of the body, voice, emotions, and physicality. In this case the identity of "good [girl] student" may have ensured Thea's initial participation in the study. It also may have made it more difficult for her and the others to directly challenge what was asked of them.

Although a "Math person," Thea has some interest in reading and writing but, evidently, it was not a passion in her life as it was for Rebecca. Thea mentioned that she kept a journal and that she wrote letters to friends. In contrast to the others in the study, Thea stated that she didn't experience much difficulty with school writing assignments: "I've never had a problem with it. I actually enjoy it, even if the assignment is stupid." Thea did take pleasure in reading. Over spring break she read Jane Austen's *Pride and Prejudice* and "really, really liked it." In her journal she wrote: "I love the kinds of books that you just can't put down. . . . I stayed up until 2 a.m. trying to finish *Jane Eyre* and read two of the *Vampire Chronicles* for five hours straight." Her reading material, as suggested in the titles she cited, was varied, a fact she confirmed later: "I read basically everything but sci-fi."

Despite the enjoyment she experienced in her reading and writing, Thea also said repeatedly that these activities were not especially important pastimes in what she described as a very busy life. She wrote, "On my own time, I rarely write. It's not often I have spare time and when I do, there are many things I enjoy doing and writing is not really one of them" and then later in the same entry she commented slightly more positively, "I wish I had more time to read or write but not anymore than wanting more time to bake or watch T.V. or knit or sleep, etc."

Over the duration of the study, Thea submitted ten pages of journal entries, and four poems totalling 114 lines. She also submitted a portfolio of poems that she had previously written for her creative writing class. It was her own idea to share her portfolio. Initially she wrote at some length in her journal, responding to questions I had asked. Over time her journal writing decreased, but she continued to submit poetry with some commentary about her poems attached. She conscientiously read all the materials and attempted, at least initially, to write within the demands of the study. Not only did she read all the poems we studied as a group in the sessions but, unlike the other girls, also read optional poems for personal reading.

Thea attended regularly until the third-last session of the study when she asked to rejoin her creative writing class. The reason she gave at that time was that her school work was suffering as a result of the time required by the research, and the study had already run over the time initially set for it, which was quite true. She did participate in the individual interviews at the very end of the study. At that time I asked her about her decision to leave the project. She reiterated the problems she had with the extended time of the study and further commented, "I volunteered for this thing because basically Betty did. She [Betty] was in the class and then she transferred classes and so then I was there and I didn't know anyone else in the group, and just personal preference. I just preferred to stay in class because we were getting marks on that and not this."[1] I asked her if the material had offended her. She replied, "Well it didn't really enlighten me that much, but it didn't offend me." I asked her whether she had gained anything from the study and she answered, "Not really. I think I would have preferred to stay in class."

This was a somewhat predictable answer considering Thea's reason for volunteering for the study, the extent of her interest in creative writing, and most importantly, her strong views and attitudes about feminism, literature, and schooling that she expressed over the course of the study. While, in my estimation, there is a softness in the tone of her journal writing and creative writing, in class Thea sometimes challenged sharply, assertively, and intelligently the positions, views, and assumptions made by myself or others in the class. She did not engage in extended discussion about her views, at least during class, but simply offered brief questions or comments.

What became apparent over the study was that Thea held or at least expressed views and opinions that were diametrically opposed to many of the premises of feminist avant-garde writing. Unlike the others, she was much more likely to directly if just briefly express her views. It was an oppositional position that she held on to tenaciously, and I suspect, a position that made it increasingly difficult for her to participate in the research project. She, like the other students, refused the premises and pleasures of the feminist literature, and refused identification with the "woman" produced in feminist avant-garde literature. The particular investments or commitments that seemed to secure her refusal will be explored in this chapter. But before describing the nature and reason for her refusal, let me reiterate that Thea did manage to participate actively in the study for over two months. She complied with the demands of the study, performing the identity of the "good student" that she described. She participated, but remained, in my estimation, distant and indifferent and more openly opposed to the study than the other young women. She did not avoid or ignore the assumptions of the study and the literature offered, rather she reacted to it by seeking to distance herself through indifference and opposition.

In some sense she warned me at the outset about her distance. She commented in the first session of the study that "I'm closed about the way I feel" and her first journal entry reiterates this: "I am not much for opening up my thoughts to others." Later in the same entry, in the context of describing letter writing, she wrote, "I used to sometimes write them and end up not mailing the letter because I found the letter too revealing." In light of her reticence it was surprising how much she did speak of her personal life, and that she preferred poetry that was personal and emotional, and often wrote such poems. It was surprising, too, how involved she became in the study despite her continual claim of indifference to school, to the study, to the poetry.

Indifference as Resistance

Indifference was a common theme for Thea throughout the study. She repeatedly spoke and wrote about her indifference to school, to feminism, and to the study. In terms of school, sporadically throughout the study, and during the interview Thea commented on her frustration with teachers and schooling in general. She described high school as "just a place where you learn how to learn and that's it," and then she went on "like, when I look at what some of the teachers make us do and it's called academics and we're graded on that—I don't agree with it because some of it is wrong." She elaborated on two specific experiences: one in which students had to spend their own money for a class assignment, and another in which she was denied access to a school laboratory and as a result could not complete an assignment which had an effect on her grades. She finished with the comment: "And when I see things like that, it's just a joke. I don't care about my academics that much anymore. I can get my marks but they don't really mean anything to me." She stated further on, "I still want good marks and I'll still get good marks because I need them to get into university and not for myself anymore really."

About her creative writing class she said, "I took the class hoping I would learn something but the fact I didn't doesn't disappoint me. Like the school system is kind of like robots and stuff like that [a reference to a poem written by Janet, one of the other students in the study] but I don't mind that anymore." Evidently Thea was, at one time, personally committed to her schooling but no longer. While Thea may be exaggerating, for her, like others in the class, this research project opened up an opportunity to voice her criticisms, in particular her cynicism, about her schooling. Considering her views about school, it may not have been worth the effort to discuss or debate her ideas and opinions in the study with any great degree. Her indifference can be seen as a form of resistance to what is offered in schools. She did her school work but stayed personally detached from it. This allowed her to perform the identity of the "good student" by complying with the demands of her education and while at the same time intensely albeit passively resisting it.

Her ongoing criticism of schooling did not mean that Thea necessarily wished for change. She gave me the impression that she had found a means of coping with the conditions of schooling and did not want things to change. For example, after she complained about her creative writing class and her creative writing teacher, I asked her if and how the class could be improved, and if she would prefer her creative writing class to be more structured, which was the basis of one of her complaints. She replied, "I think I would be more stressed [if the class was improved] because I have other classes to work on. . . . [I]t makes it easy on me." During the interview I asked her about the study and what kinds of poetry I could use if I were to do it again, considering her views of the course. Twice Thea replied, "I don't know" and added, I suspect in sympathy for me: "These poems were okay for what we had to do." But I pressed: "So, you can't think of anything in particular? Thea: "No."

At times Thea defended teachers and the school system. In the opening session of the study, the students compared the pleasure and frustrations of writing for school-based assignments against those of their own personal writing. The young women used the opportunity to express with some intensity their dissatisfaction with some of their school writing assignments. They spoke about the difficulties with the time, topics, and formats required for some assignments. Thea, in opposition to the direction of the general conversation, spoke in support of teachers and of the writing done in class. She commented, "If my English teacher, if he tells us to write something—I don't have a problem with it—the length—I can usually express myself and teachers usually give you enough time to write." Despite the emptiness of the schooling experience which she fully acknowledged, Thea seemed to defend the work required since she could comply easily and successfully with the demands of the assignments.

Apart from her grades, what perhaps sustained Thea from the emptiness of her education may have been her school friends. She described at one point how during her creative writing class her teacher had said, "how a lot of people just come to school for the social events, and that's true. They just come for lunch and I come to have fun and I don't want the summer to come because I won't see anyone, you know. I don't find anything wrong with that." The slippage from "they" to "I" was telling. For Thea the presence of her friends made school life important.

The social environment of school and the grades attached to assignments made school experience meaningful for Thea. Her cynicism and indifference to learning countered the optimism and idealism that inform the possibilities for change offered in feminist literature or any effort at educational reform. Indifference and cynicism ensures that no change will occur. The question is what was placed at risk in the literature and subject position(s) offered in the feminist writing; What was fuelling this threatening? Like Rebecca, Thea's response to the explicit marking of gender and race in feminist avant-garde literature revealed much about what was, or more precisely, who was, placed in jeopardy.

Marking Gender: Refusing the "Female Stuff"

Like the other students in the study, Thea found the emphasis on "female stuff" in the readings objectionable. She tended to conflate any emphasis on women with feminism. Her first comment in the seminars was to ask if all the poets in the study were feminists and repeatedly over the course of the study, she asked about men writing avant-garde poetry. In her second entry Thea wrote that she was finding it difficult to write for the study because, "I'm really not liking the topics of the poems and am not really inspired to write after reading them" and then followed directly with the statement, "I'm not a feminist or even remotely close." In the next class I thought we should begin by talking about feminism. We began with Rebecca's statement: "I think I should let you know that I'm not a feminist. I believe that almost all men are scum and that every woman should have every right, but I don't follow or have any wish to follow all of the feminist issues." After some of the other girls had spoken in response to Rebecca's opinion, indicating that they found feminists too extreme, Thea commented, "I am not a feminist. I don't find anything wrong with the guys I know. I am very indifferent and passive. I don't care about equal rights, wages. I would be completely happy to grow up and get married and be a housewife. I would love that. I am just indifferent towards it all."

Coming to the defense of her male friends, Thea refused a feminist politics, distancing herself dramatically by her statement, "I am just indifferent towards it all." While both Rebecca and Thea took up the work of this study seriously and conscientiously, both refused a feminist identity. Thea's views, stated with great conviction, I might add, made it all the more difficult to take up the issue with her. This may have indeed been the point. Not only was Thea defending her male friends in the quotation cited above, she was also carefully forging and defending connections among femininity, passivity, pleasure, and heterosexuality. She insisted on a desire to be happy, married (heterosexual), and passive. This identity as passive female is not available in the feminist literature, nor perhaps in the set of literature chosen was there the possibility of acknowledging one's pleasure in men. My continued assurances that one could be a feminist and be married did not convince Thea or leave her any less indifferent or negative about feminist literature.

In her interview Thea reiterated her objections to the exclusive focus on women in the study:

> Thea: But the point of a whole bunch of females getting together
> and reading poems about themselves it's just— [she doesn't finish]
> Helen: That's upsetting.
> Thea: Why can't everyone do it—that's what I don't understand . . .
> the fact we were divided. I didn't like it.

Later in the interview, Thea commented again, "I don't see women and men differently: just people writing."

Like Rebecca, Thea was quite adamant in her refusal to mark gender and in her insistence on "people." The one and only time she wavered occurred during the interview when we were discussing a poem about violence against women.

> Thea: I think there is violence everywhere. The fact there is violence
> against women and a group of women writers and for us, a bunch of
> girls studying—that is all so female that it just— [she doesn't finish]
> Helen: Makes you sick.
> Thea: Yeah.
> Helen: It's too female?
> Thea: No, it emphasized that it was a female thing. . . . But it's not
> because there's violence everywhere but because that's all we were given
> that, that—[she doesn't finish]
> Helen: It seems too narrow.
> Thea: Yeah.
> Helen: I think of it as protection—one out of four women confront
> this.
> Thea: For me, I don't think we need protection. I guess maybe I'm
> narrow-minded in a sense—only thinking of me.

Evidently Thea had not been directly affected by gender oppression or felt the fear of male violence or, perhaps and more likely, she had, but was not admitting or naming it as such to me. But in response to my statistic, she was willing this one time to say that her experience might be narrow and that there might be women whose lives were not like hers. While some women or in Thea's words "people" may experience discrimination she herself had not, and, since she is evidently not oppressed in her own life, she did not need the "protection" of feminist knowledge and women-only groups.

Thea's insistence on naming herself as passive or indifferent seemed contradictory. To me she seemed very assertive during the course of the study. Her self-description may be context specific. She named herself as passive and indifferent following her comment that there was nothing wrong with the male friends she had and that she was not a feminist. This statement together with her refusal to name "male" violence allowed Thea to insist on passivity and indifference because men pose no threat, no danger. To mark gender, particularly in the area of male violence, is to potentially turn men into enemies rather than friends (and possibly boyfriends although Thea did not mention this). Despite my insistence that this need not happen—that one could be a housewife and be a feminist—Thea was not reassured. Thea's insistence on passivity was possible because "there is nothing wrong with the guys" she knew. Her indifference towards feminism is a function of Thea's belief in her own agency in the world, and, related to this, her trust in men.

The emphasis in this study on female readers, and writers, and on gender oppression disrupts an identity based on individuality and agency. It disrupts the desire to see oneself as powerful in the world, and to see men as "safe," posing no special threat because of their gender, and therefore unproblematic as friends and lovers. Disruption of this identity and its investments occurs not only in the marking of gender but also of race.

Marking Race

Thea's refusal to highlight gender difference during the study extended to race as well. With some notable exceptions, Thea did not mark herself racially during the research project. Several reasons became apparent during her interview. At the end of the interview, almost as an aside, I mentioned to her that I noticed the school was very multiracial, and then asked her whether she had ever been the target of discrimination. She replied, "No, not seriously" and then talked at some length about the acceptance she felt within her group of white friends.

Thea: A lot of my friends are white. I think I'm the only Oriental that really hangs around with them. And I'm friends with G—but I prefer my white friends and it's not because they're white. People like T—in

our writing class jokingly says I'm whitewashed. . . .I say I'm yellow
and he says I'm urine colored, but I mean it's a joke. He doesn't mean
it and he's my friend and I'm not offended by that. But I've never been
seriously discriminated against.
Helen: So you identify as an Asian woman?
Thea: Yes like when he says, I'm whitewashed and really meant it, I
would be really offended but I know he is just joking and he knows that
it would offend me. . . .I would be very insulted if someone I didn't
know called me white.

But although her racial and ethnic background was obviously
very important to Thea, and important to acknowledge personally, it
was an identity that she did not need to have acknowledged publicly
in school curriculum. Thea was adamant about this, as the following
segment from her interview indicates:

Helen: Does it bother you then, if you identify yourself as Asian, to
look at an English curriculum and find there are no Asian women
represented?
Thea: No, that's just what I don't like about the women doing the I am
a feminist thing, you know.
Helen: You don't think it's important that Asian-Canadians be represented on the English curriculum or in the history or—
Thea: No, I'm in Canada.
Helen: Yeah but there are Asian Canadians.
Thea: No.
Helen: It doesn't bother you that Asian-Canadian women are producing
tremendous amounts of poetry and short stories now, it's coming out in
volumes just now, that that hasn't somehow trickled down to high
schools?
Thea: No, it doesn't offend me at all. The only difference I see between
myself and everyone else is how we are raised. Korean culture is dif-
ferent. I don't know how to explain it because you're not Korean.
Helen: So it doesn't bother you that there are no Asian-Canadians
represented in the curriculum.
Thea: I wouldn't even notice it.
Helen: Now that I've pointed it out, would it bother you?
Thea: No. I'm Korean by the way I behave.

Evidently there are conditions under which Thea will mark race
and more specifically herself as Korean, or Asian-Canadian, but this

does not include in school curriculum and perhaps more generally in the public sphere. She marked a difference in the private sphere—in how children are raised in the home, but she would not extend that further, refusing the opportunity to mark gender and race available in the feminist avant-garde literature. It is possible that she was refusing the particular marking of race offered in feminist literature. It was clear that Thea did not want her Korean identity lost. She would be offended if someone accused her of being white, or of being "white-identified," but she did not want a Korean identity high-lighted in the school.

The marking of gender and race in the feminist avant-garde literature of this study was in direct opposition to what Thea understood and was comfortable with. Clearly her views were placed in jeopardy by the explicit marking of race in school curriculum. The costs for Thea in underscoring difference rather than universality were too high. Her last comments in the interview named these costs:

> Thea: I see it [the curriculum] more universal. . . .I don't think it should be that divided. [She then suddenly started talking about the Black Music Awards.] Why do they [Black artists] have to have their own separate one [awards]?
> Helen: But who's been winning [music] awards but white writers and performers.
> Thea: But it leaves us so divided.

"But it leaves us so divided"—this last statement, her last statement in the study, is haunting. I share Thea's concern about a focus on difference that might lead only to unbridgeable divisions among individuals and groups of individuals. But unlike me, Thea strongly believed that attention to universal experience would override any gender or racial difference, keeping everyone together. This belief in the universal experience or the core humanity for Thea may create or allow a generic identity that ensures easy acceptance by white friends and/or male friends. The danger in mentioning or acknowledging social difference particularly as it relates to gender and racial oppression is that it may taint or disrupt the dreams and desires for unproblematic relationships across difference. And perhaps this was the danger of mentioning sexism and racism, of putting women and oppression in the same sentence, for Thea and for the other young women—a problem of connection. It was thus difficult for them to work with feminist literature and its deliberate marking of gender and at times race.

Writing Poetry: Attention to Form

Considering the views Thea articulated, it was not surprising that she was so negative about the study, yet she did stay in the class until the last month, producing a considerable amount of writing in the process. This was all the more remarkable since feminist avant-garde literature demands attention to literary form and language convention, and this, too, was difficult for Thea. In her second journal entry she commented on the difficulty she was experiencing writing. As quoted earlier, Thea wrote that she was not inspired by the topics of the poems and went on to say, "I also found it hard to copy a form of poetry. Usually when I write poems it's when I want to express my thoughts but not straight out. So when I write poetry, usually I'm just writing down what I feel and so I'm not really thinking about the form that it's taking but rather the words that I'm using." The stress on thoughts and feelings over the form and language conventions reflects and supports a psychological model of creative writing as described in previous chapters. It was a model supported in her creative writing class.

Thea tried to work within the feminist literature, although it was difficult and ultimately unsatisfying. Thea identified this in the first writing she did for the study. She, like Rebecca, chose to write using the form of the poem, "the hairdresser" "because that seemed the easiest." She used her lunchtime conversation among her friends in the school cafeteria as a topic and wrote the poem in block style. Her poem was entitled "Lunchtime" and a section of it reads:

> Someone save my seat? Someone nods John gets up. Sue studies her chemistry Kim tells me what's on the french test I try to read the story Paul says we should do our homework at home we bore him talk about the weekend if it's Friday and again on Monday Steph eats a revelle eighty-six cents gossip about her gossip about him about the both of them cold curly fries, oatmeal muffins, ice tea of course want a sweet tart two o'clock see you in french.

Although myself and others in the class thought the poem was very successful in emulating the form and style of "the hairdresser," Thea did not like her poem, and said, "had I written it without thinking about the form, I think I would have split it into separate lines. But then I wouldn't write about lunch on my own anyway." She repeatedly told me of how hollow the experience of writing the poem was, and that she was simply complying with the demands of the study. She stated, "I was indifferent to "lunchtime". There was nothing on my mind. I just wrote it because I had to write it—I was told to write it." In the interview she commented, "I just did it because it was an assignment."

In her first poem, Thea, like Rebecca, attempted to emulate the form of a poem given in class, but disappointed with her first effort, she did not try to do so again. She refused the feminist literature. She told me that in her second poem she wrote more in her "own style." She wrote in her journal, "Looking Deeper" [her second poem] is more typical of what I'd normally write. In fact I wrote it without even thinking about this class or the poems that we read on Thursday." Ignoring the study, she wrote a poem that was highly personal and evidently autobiographical and most importantly was spontaneously produced. She commented, "I was just distraught, I guess, and angry over something and so I wrote it. I wasn't thinking about what kind of form it was taking or anything. I was just writing it." The poem suggests a betrayal in a personal relationship and the loneliness and alienation that results.

> Don't listen with prejudice;
> don't speak with ignorance.
> Don't ask me what's wrong,
> while inflicting the pain.
> Don't tell me you love me,
> while you're with another. . . .
>
> in this world
> We are constantly surrounded by others
> unable to escape them
> and yet,
> utterly and unbearably
> alone.
>
> You do not know me.

Although all the characters in her first poem are identified as students, there are no social markers, no context here. It feels as though as Thea wrote for herself alone and then offered to share this piece with me. It is so personal that it is difficult to know what has happened. I found it uncomfortable to read, as I did with much of the writing the young women submitted. It seemed to require a nurturing, therapeutic response to the writer's emotional state rather than a response to the content and form of the writing itself and social context and discourses that inform the writing. Many times I felt compelled to respond to their writing in the mode of a counselor. It became difficult and often inappropriate to move to comments on literary form and innovation in the work produced.

The position of counselor may have been a result of the specific conditions of the study. Since there were only six students I had a great deal of interaction with each of them. I had access to their thoughts and feelings from their creative writing, journals, classroom discussions, and individual interviews for a period of nearly three months. Neither their teacher nor their parent, I was located outside of the fray of those relationships. As an outsider to these relationships, and as a concerned adult and keen researcher intensely interested in what they had to say, the students may have felt more comfortable with me and more likely to share aspects of their personal lives. They well may have enjoyed the attention they were given. In some sense the students were lured into providing personal responses by the conditions of the study and the intense researcher-participant relationship it sets into play. The danger of qualitative research is that participants are placed in some emotional risk since the researcher's primary interest in them lies in the collection of data, although certainly I grew to like and care about the students in my study. Obviously a responsible researcher needs to be conscious of the effects of this relationship and of a responsibility to participants with regard to the emotional risks, in particular the effects of disclosure that are inherent in the very nature of qualitative research.

It is also important to mention here that if poetry is understood and organized as a highly personal and emotional literary form, it then creates the conditions for students to share personal and private emotions and thoughts in their writing. Since Thea, by her own admission, used poetry to explore her thoughts and feelings, it was not surprising that the poetry she produced for the study was highly personal. Furthermore if her schooling supported this view of poetry then her writing would not seem unusual.

Despite Thea's insistence that form was not at all important in her poetry, there were moments when she acknowledged her interest in the form. At one point, she showed me an earlier draft of her second poem in which she had written small numbers beside the lines. She explained that she wanted the poem to fit on one page and so was counting the lines. She commented, "[T]hings like that bother me because I'm a perfectionist." She wanted the poem to fit the page perfectly. I asked her why she had indented and then dropped a line to put the word "alone" by itself on the line. She replied, "I don't know why I did that. I wasn't conscious of it." While Thea, as a perfectionist, attended to the aesthetic look of the poem on the page, she refused to become conscious or describe herself as conscious, of the form of the poem in any other regard. She did not want to be deliberate (or appear deliberate) in her use of literary form and language conventions, and so refused this tenet of feminist avant-garde writing. The question is why not: what intellectual and affective investments would have been disrupted or challenged for Thea had she been deliberate in her choices of literary form and convention.

As mentioned in Chapter One, the attention to language and literary form in feminist avant-garde is connected to the socio-political nature of writing and the writing subject. It is possible that Thea was refusing the notion of writing a consciously crafted and, more specifically, as a deliberate political act. In the context of this research, Thea's comments served to reestablish an identity of the writer as one who focuses on emotions and thoughts oblivious to form and social context. It was unclear in this instance why this identity of writer was so important to her. However, there were clues in her comments about marking gender and race, and in her poetry.

Thea's poem "Looking Deeper" and Rebecca's poem "Inner Debate," are thematically similar. Both focus on loneliness and alienation. Thea's lines, for example, "We are constantly surrounded by others/ unable to escape them/ and yet,/ utterly and unbearably/ alone" echo strangely with Rebecca's lines "I feel lost sometimes sometimes?/ a lot/ You think you're alone/ I am alone/ purposely/ I don't know, I don't think so. . . .You can't relate to people, can you/they can't relate to me." The young women in this study often wrote about loneliness.

In light of Thea's concern with social divisiveness, specifically of the importance of her relationships with her white friends and her male friends, it may be that by engaging the literature in this project, Thea and other students were reminded of, or confronted with, the possibility that their relationships with others may not result in some perfect union—that relationships are problematic. This in turn may have reinforced or produced a sense of isolation already present in the discursive formation and material conditions of adolescents in the late twentieth century. The emphasis on individualism, personal agency, and independence that underlies much of the liberalism of North American society no doubt contributes to a sense of isolation among students, as desirable as those qualities might be to them. They are lonely. Forced to reject identity politics by a desire to ensure the viability of a connection and union with "the other" and perhaps knowing the tenuousness of that connection, and supported by a more familiar construction of creative writing that emphasizes the personal, the psychological, the therapeutic, students wrote poetry that speaks of isolation and loneliness.

The attention to literary form and language convention, the specification of gender and race, and the assumption of oppression in feminist avant-garde writing disrupts the dream of the perfect connection or union with others. However, it is not connection with just anyone that is at risk but rather relationships with men and white people for Thea, and with men and people of color for Rebecca. At risk are relationships with those who could be seen as "different from me" or "other."

The feminist literature did not threaten a desire for connection to women. The students seemed to find it easier or less risky to write about relationships among women—a topic that many of the students, including Thea, chose to write about, with great enthusiasm, I might add. Thea, having refused feminist avant-garde writing in her second poem, suddenly turned back to the literature for the theme of her third poem. In class we read and discussed Bronwen Wallace's poem "Between Words," a poem for and about the experiences of a nurse, "Carole," (who is represented as Wallace's friend) and the young women Carole sees coming in for their "yearly babies." A strong connection is created between the young women, the narrator, and the readers of the poem. In class I emphasized, among other things, this connectedness or blurring between woman as reader, writer, and subject of the poem. Thea used this poem as inspiration to write about her friend Caroline. In one of the few positive comments Thea made about the study, she wrote, "I liked how 'Between Words' was directed towards Carole. That it was for her alone. So then I thought about how I could use that. Well, I thought of Caroline because she's a good friend of mine and at the moment she's the only one I would want to direct a poem to."

The poem Thea wrote was again highly personal, speaking about events that could only be fully understood by Caroline.

> Remember the time you slept over?
> We stayed up late
> roasting marshmallows in the microwave
> and watching Porkies on T.V.
> or Korea in '86
> When you cried so they would house us together
> and that storm with the psycho lady
> and how I scared you completely
> and how we threw a popsicle wrapper out the
>   window
> just to see where it would land
> or last winter
> When we took a walk
> and compared you to the yellow insulated wire
> that stood out;
> that didn't belong;
> in the "perfect winter forest scene"
> that fell around us.
>
> The picture, Caroline,
> is not what hangs on the wall in front of me
> Because when I look at that 5 by 7
> on its frameless frame
> I don't see the two girls smiling
> but everything else
>
> It's not just black and white.

The feminist literature provided Thea with an opportunity to write about female friendships and she seized the opportunity as did others in the study. Perhaps Thea was able to take up this theme because she saw an opportunity to write about meaningful relationships between women without invoking notions of gender oppression. It is telling, I think, that in this poem Thea identifies herself and her friend as female, as "two girls smiling." It would seem that Thea can mark gender in this instance since to speak of women does not reference men and/or gender oppression. It does not threaten relationships with men. But although she mentions gender, she also seems to write it away: "I don't see the two girls smiling but everything else. It's not just black and white." According to Thea, black and white here refers to a black and white photograph, and she is using the expression to indicate the depth and complexity of the relationship she has with Caroline—that it is rich with memory and detail and color (?). I am not sure whether Caroline is Korean or not, but I suspect she is from what Thea writes in the poem. The "yellow wire" might well have been a reference to race. In my written comments to the poem I asked why her friend was compared to "a yellow insulated wire that stood out and didn't belong," but Thea did not answer the question. I suspect she would not have acknowledged or named race as significant in this poem. However, supported by the feminist literature, what Thea was able to do in this poem was describe the joy she experienced in her friendship to Caroline.

The verses and line length vary considerably in this poem. Thea allowed herself to play a bit more in regard to form. In her last poem she experimented more with form, drawing on Libby Oughton's poem "so i'm afraid of getting what i want?" a poem that featured multiple narrative voices. The poem Thea wrote was entitled, " Talk Me Back Down to the Ground" and, as she described it, the poem had two voices speaking at the opening and at the end, and "a poem in the middle." There is little context provided in this poem and nothing that identifies the writer or characters. A section of the poem reads as follows:

> Why?
> Because.
> Why Because
> Just Because
> Just because
>
> Frantically searching for answers
> Without even knowing the questions
> and not knowing where to look

> I was scared
> I was having a bad dream
> But you weren't sleeping. . . .
> I know
> I was wide awake.

In her journal Thea admitted she wasn't sure what this poem was about. "I don't really know what it was that I was writing about." But she offered some sort of analysis: "I suppose if I were to analyze it myself, it would be about someone who is confused and I guess frustrated with life. The bad dream being life itself. But that's sort of wrong because I wasn't feeling that way when I wrote it and I usually I write what I feel. I guess this time I didn't." Thea attempted to make sense of what she has written by focusing on her own emotional state at the time, emphasizing the psychological use of poetry.

Despite having used a form from one of the poems, Thea re-iterated several times during the interview and during the project that form wasn't significant to her. She stated, "Basically when I write I just don't really think of form or anything. When you introduce these things to us it was just, oh—it didn't do anything for me because I never even thought that they were really different. To me they were just poems. I didn't notice anything different from them." Evidently she did notice something different about them, for I asked about referring to the works as poems and she replied "they're all creative writing and literature—not poems. I don't know—I would call them stories." She went on to say, "I would call it writing. Whether it's a poem or not, it's writing." There was obviously some confusion for Thea on this point. It seems that the feminist writing was not that different in terms of its form yet it was not really poetry. Although Thea didn't say more, I suspect some of the difficulty for her rested in finding a way to avoid naming the work as poetry, so as to keep intact her particular notion of poetry. If form was not the determining factor in what Thea regarded as poetry, then it may have been content that was crucial. Since the focus of the poetry was on "female stuff," I would speculate that Thea, like some literary critics, may have thought that writing depicting the specific experiences of women was too narrow to be considered "literature" or "poetry."

In light of Thea's views on literature, feminism and identity, it strikes me now that the kind of pedagogical intervention I offered in this study was not at all appropriate for her. Rather than offering poetry by and about women, I should have offered her rereadings of "the classics" that made problematic the notion of the "universal" experience depicted in literature. I am not sure that she would have accepted such readings, but I think it might have been a more useful place to begin. Instead the strongest intervention I made with Thea was to give her a poem written by a contemporary Japanese woman writer that used a photograph as a central image and so was similar in some ways to her poem "It's Not Just Black and White." At the time I wasn't sure about doing it and now, in light of what she said during the study and particularly in the interview, it was probably the worst thing I could have done. Predictably, Thea ignored the poem and its explicit marking of Asian women, refusing the feminist avant-garde literature.

Conclusion

Feminist avant-garde literature demands attention to literary form, language convention, and to issues of social difference, specifically gender oppression. Because of her investment in the identity of a "good student," Thea attempted to satisfy the demand of the study. But she resisted the attention to literary form and social difference, negotiating against these premises. The kind of literary and writing experience and the subject position of woman the study offered her was largely unacceptable and undesirable to Thea, and prompted indifference towards the study and an insistence on more traditional views about literature and writing. Part of what seemed to underpin Thea's negotiations was a concern that highlighting difference and social inequality might threaten relationships with her male and white friends. In particular, heterosexual desire forged in feminine passivity and pleasure was placed at risk. The psychologically based progressive model of creative writing and the transcendent identity of the writer that it produces certainly appears far "safer" and, for Thea, not worth changing.

Two Samples of Thea's Poems

The Black and White
(for Caroline)

It hangs on the wall above my desk
the 5 by 7 in its frameless frame
We must've took ten shots at least
just to guarantee a good one
and you made me crouch
just so you wouldn't look so short
that's why he shot above the waist.

Remember the time you slept over?
We stayed up late, roasting
marshmallows in the microwave
and watching Porkies on TV.

or Korea in '86
When you cried so they would house
us together
and that storm with the psycho lady
and how I scared you completely
and how we threw a popsicle wrapper
out the window
just see where it would land.

or last winter
when we took a walk
and compared you to the yellow
insulated wire
that stood out,
that didn't belong,
in the "perfect winter forest scene"
that fell all around us.

The picture Caroline,
is not what hangs on the wall in front
of me
Because when I look at that 5 by 7
in its frameless frame
I don't see the two girls smiling
but everything else.

Looking Deeper

Don't listen with prejudice
don't speak with ignorance
Don't ask me what's wrong
while inflicting the pain.
Don't tell me you love me,
while you're with another
Don't smile and laugh,
if you're feeling miserable inside
Don't look with unopened eyes,
Don't think with a narrow mind.

There is something out there
and within you and me
It is real
and greater than
anything you could imagine.

For what you imagine
of me, for example,
of what I am
of who I am
of what I want to be
Is only your interpretation
of what I reveal
and may not be really me
if it is prejudged or seen with ignorance.

In this world
we are constantly surrounded by others
unable to escape them
and yet,
utterly and unbearably
alone.

You do not know me.

Chapter Five

Threatening the Rebel

Janet

I don't like being told what to do.
That's for everything not just writing.
                    —one of the first things Janet says

Helen: Which one [poem from the study] do you
really like now?
Janet: I like the ones that have swearing in them.
(she laughs)
Helen: Why?
Janet: 'Cause it's something that school doesn't allow.
                    —from her interview

At the time of the study Janet was a seventeen-year-old student enrolled in the same creative writing class as the other young women in the study. Although she enjoyed her creative writing class, she was not, by her own account, an avid reader or writer. She admitted, "I'm not a big reading person." Although not an avid reader, Janet could become quite enthusiastic about some of the literature she read for school assignments. For example, she described Dylan Thomas's poem "Do Not Go Gently Into That Good Night," saying, "I loved it. That was a wicked poem. It's powerful." She described "Fear," a poem from the study, with similar enthusiasm, "It was powerful. It stands in your throat. It just keeps banging on you."

Janet mentioned that she enjoyed writing short stories, but, unlike Rebecca, she did not write in her spare time. She didn't like "doing [school] stuff" on her own time. However, Janet did not view all writing as bound up with school practices. She admitted that she wrote songs for her own pleasure. According to her comments in class her current boyfriend played in a heavy metal band and wrote music, and she, too, tried her hand at writing songs. This may have provided an alternative experience and notion of writing from that generated in school-based purposes and practices.

Janet was unusual in the group in that she identified herself as someone who experienced a great deal of difficulty with school and school authority. She was not a good student. Janet could not or would not easily comply with the demands of teachers. During our first meeting, she attributed the difficulties she had experienced with writing assignments to her problems with authority. She told me at the start of the study, perhaps as a warning: "I don't like being told what to do. That's for everything, not just writing." This was not said in a hostile manner but dispassionately, as information. Janet frequently and very blatantly expressed her loathing of teachers both in what she said and wrote. During her interview she commented, "And teachers, I don't know, I think they're wrong half the time anyway so it's hard. It's easier to take opinions from people you respect and I, honestly, I don't trust a lot of these teachers."

Since Janet would not easily comply with the demands of high school life, regardless of the consequences, her school career was threatened. At the time of the study she was failing English and planning to quit school as soon as the academic year was finished, provided she wasn't suspended first. She was quite concerned about school suspension, as she indicated in her journal, "I have to keep reminding myself that I'm going to graduate and getting myself suspended will not get me out of here [school] any earlier." As it turned out, despite her feelings about teachers and schooling, Janet would not be finished entirely with formal education at the end of the school year. At the end of the study she informed me that she had enrolled in a three-year broadcasting course at a local community college.

Despite her general attitude toward schooling and teachers, and perhaps because of it, Janet participated enthusiastically in the study.

She produced six poems totalling 106 lines and four short (1/2 page) journal entries. She attended regularly and participated actively in class discussion. Indeed she was very outspoken. During the interview Janet remarked that she had enjoyed "the talking we did." She seemed to take up seriously the ideas in the poems selected for the study and often referred to ideas or poems discussed in previous sessions.

From my observations, the poems and journal entries Janet submitted appeared to be first drafts, hastily written, usually during class time. This was quite unlike the kind of lengthy and conscientiously written and redrafted pieces of writing submitted by Rebecca and the others. Janet's poems and journal entries look and read as though they were written on impulse. I suspect they were. Although she did submit written work, Janet seemed to prefer to voice her ideas and opinions orally. Near the end of the study, she indicated that she had redrafted her final two poems. It is possible that Janet felt the work now worth the trouble of more focused and sustained effort on her part.

Janet used her journal entries primarily to explain the poems she had written. Since the poems were autobiographical, she did, in some instances, briefly refer to circumstances in her own life. For example, in the first entry she wrote about the poem she had just submitted:

> I wrote a poem called "Future School for Robots and Humanoids." Just in case you don't understand it, the clicking and the gears is inside the Robots who are supposed to be representing humans because we are like them in school. We do the same things over and over again. And if we come up with new ideas or argue with the views of the teacher we get stepped on.

In a later entry she writes about her poem "The! Devil! The Angel, the teacher and ME":

> Okay, I wrote this because I'm graduating this year and sometimes I feel like telling some of these stupid teachers off. But I have to keep reminding myself that I'm going to graduate and getting myself suspended will not get me out of here any earlier. So I end up biting my tongue, not wanting to get on his/her bad side.

Breaking Rules: Student Rebel

As evident in her poems, Janet depicted schooling as meaningless and monotonous, teachers as unreasonable and autocratic, and herself as a student who rebelled against them but who was often forced into silence. Three of the six poems she submitted vehemently critiqued teachers and the power inequality between teachers and students. Her first poem "Future School for Robots and Humanoids" described teachers as robots who have "empty smiles" and for whom a "question is the enemy" and "termination is the answer for a glitched circuit." Janet, it would seem, saw herself challenging teachers, "with new ideas or views" and so as a "glitched circuit" to be terminated or "suspended."

In "The! Devil! The Angel, the teacher and ME" her anger was expressed towards the fictitious teacher "Ms. Smith" who, according to Janet's comments in her journal, may well have had a real-life counterpart. Janet explained, "I wrote this because . . . I feel like telling some stupid teachers off." In this poem there was both frustration with the teacher ("the bitch") who is continually nagging, who "hasn't said anything useful yet," and with Janet's own struggle to control her anger. Her final poem, "Class," spoke about hypocritical or unreasonable school rules. Janet cited two examples in her poem. First she noted "Paper scattered all around," even though the school rule is "Remember save a tree. Use both sides of the paper." Secondly she fumed that school library books had to be returned in two days but that were impossible to finish reading in that time. In her poem the adult response to her complaints was simply "Sorry those are the rules." School rules evidently can't be violated, according to Janet, "And I can't break the rules," or her graduation would be jeopardized, at least from what she says in her journal.

Feminist avant-garde literature, and its overt breaking of literary and language rules and its acknowledgement of inequality in gender relations, gave Janet an opportunity to speak and write about the inequality and injustice she experienced in teacher-student relationships. Although none of the literature read in class directly addressed teachers and students, the research project created a space where Janet could be highly critical of teachers and schooling and depict herself as a student rebelling against the system. In all likelihood, this was not the first time that Janet produced the identity I call the "student rebel" but the themes and tenets of the literature in the study enabled Janet to reproduce the identity.

Taking the writing as autobiographical, it is evident that Janet positioned herself as a student, but not as female student, although it is interesting that the teacher was gendered: Ms. Smith. In her first poem Janet did not use first person, but according to what she wrote in her journal, the piece was to be read autobiographically. Although she was a part of the students (the "we") who will be "stepped on," in all of her other poems the student was positioned as an individual "I," not as a part of a collective. This was evident in her titles. Her first poem was entitled "Future School for Robots and Humanoids," whereas her next poem was entitled "The! Devil! The Angel, the teacher and ME," moving from robots and humanoids (students and teachers) to the "teacher and ME." The shift to more explicit and personal marking may have resulted from the fact that many of the poems in the study were written in the first person and were auto-biographical, so that there was support for such writing. While Janet used the collective "we" to refer to students, she did not refer to women collectively in her work. Janet did not directly or indirectly identify or mark herself as gendered.

While teachers in general were the focus of the poems Janet submitted, in class discussions, and in her final interview she singled out English teachers as being particularly problematic. Janet depicted English teachers as language police. During the interview, while discussing "Fear" (one of her favorites from the selections offered in the project), Janet described English teachers in this way:

Helen: Okay, so it was the images that gave "Fear" its power. Did the form affect that? Did it bother you that the lines ran like this? [pointing to the poem]
Janet: No, I think it added to it. It jumps right in your face. It's differ-rent. It catches your eye because it's all large and there is no punctu-ation. If an English teacher looked at that they would go "Ack!! XXX. Redo it."

The punctuation and the print size of the poem lay outside of what Janet believed English teachers would deem acceptable, and that unorthodox style added to the impact of the poem. She found the poem appealing because it strongly challenged the rules of English teachers. Indeed the feminist literature in general held this appeal for her. Its bold challenges to language convention corresponded to her own desire to be the student rebel boldly challenging teachers, specifically English teachers. The literature and its identity of the woman writer as actively exploring and subverting language forms and practices is like the identity of the rebel in that both are predicated on the desire to be active, bold, and oppositional to forces that oppress. Identification on such grounds was possible. Janet could continue to construct herself as the rebel even in the face of her own compliance with school rules by insisting on the overwhelming and abusive power of schools and teachers.

Janet's rebel identity in relation to English teachers was complex and surprisingly fragile, despite her words:

> I have an English teacher right now. She is very nice but the thing is, I write, really I write like this. I mix my sentences, my grammar is rotten, my spelling, so I get really lousy marks, but this teacher, on the other hand, will give me lousy marks, but then she'll come up and tell me, look you had a great idea, it's wonderful to read it, if you read it, it would be so powerful, except for you can't write. [She laughs.]

Janet quickly shifted to faulting her own abilities in language. In doing so, she reconstructed a "right" and "wrong" such that her own spelling and grammar were often faulty, in her words, "rotten." Furthermore, the comment that her teacher would give her lousy marks but still be supportive suggests that Janet did not object to the use of power (giving marks), but in the abuse of it. This was apparent at a later point in her interview when I asked about the effect of the class seminars:

> Helen: So, what would you say you got out of being in the sessions?
> Janet: An 80.
> Helen: (laughs) I didn't give marks.
> Janet: No, but Mr. C. [her creative writing teacher] did and because I was in your thing I didn't get marked for a whole bunch of stuff in his class so my mark went way up.
> Helen: Well, that's good, but what else did you get out of it?
> Janet: Really, honestly, I don't know. I had a good time.

Helen: It was fun. Did it make you think about literature differently?
Janet: Well, the only thing right now on the spot that I could say is probably that when I get stuff back that my English teacher says, "No, it's wrong." I kind of think, "Well, no you're wrong because Helen says [Janet stops and says] I think English teachers should go through this course so they can see that they should be more open-minded about it. I think that's their problem.

Although she positioned me outside of the regular mould of the English teacher, she did not denigrate or deny my power or connection with the teaching community. Although she challenged authority, Janet was also in this instance relying on it; in this last quotation it was my authority or power that she drew on to defend herself against English teachers. There is an overwhelming sense in this last quotation of the powerlessness of students in the face of narrow-minded teachers, a sense that Janet herself would not be believed without outside intervention. The student, even the rebel student, is constructed as someone very powerless, dependent on the aid of others to challenge teachers' words. There appears no difficulty for Janet in describing herself as a student who is powerless or incompetent but fighting back as the rebel.

Unlike the other young women in the study, Janet drew willingly and easily upon her experience to acknowledge the policing of literary form that takes place in schools. For her there was less risk in naming and denigrating the policing of literary forms and language conventions. Her identity as a rebel student may have made this easy to do. She did not see herself as a writer, or at least as a successful writer according to the standards of English teachers, and she could be less invested in the literary convention than Rebecca or Thea.

It was not surprising that Janet liked working in this study. Feminist avant-garde writing sanctions the breaking of language and literary conventions. It is work that celebrates the rebel. She may have found the research fun perhaps because she did not see me policing language in the same way as did her teachers. Certainly she seemed to take great delight in reading the literature in the study simply because she believed it lay outside what was considered acceptable by school authorities. Janet made this abundantly clear in a comment made during her interview:

Helen: Which one [poem] do you really like now?
Janet: I like the ones that have swearing in them. [She laughs.]
Helen: Why?
Janet: 'Cause it's something that school doesn't allow.

Good and Bad Girls

As evident in previous quotations in this chapter, Janet's speech was populated with aggressive expressions. "I go for power," she said about the poems she liked. That is, Janet liked poetry as direct and as aggressive as her own language could be. Over the course of the study she commented about the poetry she enjoyed saying, "It stands in your throat. It just keeps banging on you," and "That was a wicked poem. It's powerful." "It jumps in your face. It catches your eye. It would make a great 'thrash' song actually. You know heavy, heavy, heavy metal. Like you scream" and "If you . . . write a really powerful piece that really kicks me in the face, I would like it. This one does." Poetry for Janet should have powerful violent effects.

Although the other young women in the study "played" with poetic form and language, Janet seemed to do so much more often, more freely, and with greater pleasure. The profanity and the language play was evident in her poem "The! Devil! The Angel, the teacher and ME" which began:

> nag, nag, nag, nag, nag, nag, nag
> FUCK OFF BITCH.
> nag, nag, nag, nag, nag
> Say! It! Out! Loud! Stupid!

Similarly, Janet's poem "Child of Love" began:

> No good, lousy, son of a bitch
> get a brain,
> get a job,
> get a life!
> You R No GOOD!!!

Janet was not merely breaking rules at random. Students were to choose one of the techniques used in the poems studied and incorporate the technique however they wished in their own writing. The first poem we read and discussed, Joy Parks' "Rhymes to Grow By," contained profanity. I did not describe it as a technique for use in their own writing, but Janet seized the opportunity perhaps to test the bounds of what was allowable rule-breaking. The play with punctuation, capitalization, letter script, and the use of common rhymes and sayings evident in Janet's writing all occurred in the poems we studied in class. Clearly Janet was breaking conventions using the poems. There was a sense of zeal in her efforts to break with conventions that wasn't apparent with the other students. Her attitudes towards school and English teachers no doubt contributed to her enthusiasm for the assignment.

Perhaps because she liked the poems "with swearing in them," her poems contained profanity, although surprisingly her oral speech, did not. According to her comments in her journal her poem, "The! Devil! The Angel, the teacher and ME" depicted a struggle between the "good" and "evil" sides of her nature. The "evil" side, presumably the devil of her title, wanted Janet to tell the teacher to "Fuck off Bitch" and encouraged her to "say it out loud Stupid" and to "Kill her Stupid!" This aggressive, violent speech was quite unlike what I heard or read from others in the study, even when they were frustrated or angry.

Constructing herself as "bad girl" at least some of the time, Janet predictably spoke more openly about sex and relationships with men. During one session she talked about flirting, "I flirt with all my guy friends. They flirt with me. I have so many fake dates lined up it's not funny." She spoke often about her boyfriend and in one of her poems commented that she and her best friend Selena "share men," although I am not sure what she means by that phrase:

> Selena talks listens cares shares
> double dates shopping trips shared sports
> shared men shared dinner.

There was much support for the "bad girl" in this study. The poetry selected for the seminars supported notions of alternative re-presentations of women and girls that lie outside what is conventional. The unconventional was often associated with the "bad" or "dangerous" woman. The first poem in the study, "Rhymes to Grow By," was in fact a celebration of the "bad girl" played off the sweetness and innocence of children's nursery rhymes. It was a poem

Janet greatly enjoyed. She was obviously delighted with the poem
when it was read, listed it as one of her favorites, and mentioned it
during her interview: "It was funny the way they twisted all these little
children's rhymes." Janet identified strongly with the image of the
"bad" girl growing up. After commenting on the twisting of rhymes,
Janet spoke of her own childhood:

> It's funny. Like even just like last night, at the dinner table, we [she
> and her brother] were sitting with our parents and my mom was saying,
> do you remember when this and this, and you were so cute. She was
> telling me about something about school. And all I remember is some
> guy, and wrapping a [undiscernible] and pulling it and making his nose
> bleed. And she [her mother] remembers, "oh you used to skip with all
> the little boys" and I remember beating them up. It's a different view, I
> don't know.

It is interesting that Janet didn't discount her mother's view. She
described it as "different," not wrong. She shifted slightly here—a
bad girl but from another point of view, a girl who was "so cute." It
is possible that Janet did not discount her mother's view because of
the respect she held for her. Janet spoke several times about her
mother, specifically about how she and her mother had so reasonably
negotiated Janet's curfew time. The pseudonym that she chose for the
study (Janet) was her mother's name. It is also possible that Janet was
reluctant to so narrowly define herself as "the bad girl" or as the
"rebel" because there were limits to the rules she would break and to
the unconventionality she would adopt. The limits to her identification with feminist avant-garde writing became evident as the study
continued.

Although Janet broke the rules of being a "good girl" by writing
contemptuously of teachers and of schooling, and enjoyed works that
broke with convention, there were limits to the rules she would tamper
with, to what she would accept as poetry, and to what she would
tolerate from feminism. Over the course of the project it became clear
what and where her limits were. Janet did enjoy breaking with literary
and language convention. "I had a good time" she said about the
study, "I like getting a chance to do something weird. I write bizarre

stuff usually." Despite claiming to enjoy unconventional literature, the poem "Shock Troop" irritated her.

> Janet: Do you have "Shock Troop"?. . . . It's dumb. It's dumb.
> Helen: Why is it dumb?
> Janet: Because all they did, it sounds like, like, they just threw these words together. They randomly picked them out of a hat and stuck them on paper and said, "ta da! I want 500 dollars for this poem please". . . The author just wanted a quick buck.

For Janet a poem should conform to the conventional meanings of words so that it is at least readable to the audience. Although she did break some rules, Janet did not wish to break this rule in her own writing, although evidently she tried. She wrote in her journal:

> After reading "Shock Troop" I figured I could write a whole bunch of gibberish and call it poetry. But I couldn't do it. I started to write "Child of Love" but different styles started poping [sic] in and working. So when I finished it I started again with "Class" but again different styles popped in and I liked it.

According to her journal her attempt to write in a similar fashion to "Shock Troop" failed, but the process seemed to permit different styles to "pop" into what she had previously written. This was the only time she redrafted the work she was doing. The poem that clearly disgusted her: "I HATED SHOCK TROOP," she wrote on a list of her most and least favorite poems in the project, yet it seemed to prompt her to rework her own writing.

The kinds of "styles that pop in" to Janet's poems "Child of Love" and "Class" broke conventional rules of capitalization, punctuation, line and verse format. But although Janet was breaking language and literary standards, in terms of theme, the poetry in the project did not offer a particularly enticing place from which to write for Janet or the others. While Janet could produce "the bad girl" or "the rebel" by breaking language convention, and in condemning teachers and schooling, issues of gender did not filter into her work. Indeed, while endorsing feminism to some degree, Janet largely refused the kind of rule-breaking opportunities it offered with regard to gender.

Following Rules

Janet, like the other young women in the study, generally refused the explicit marking of gender. This became apparent in the second class when I introduced feminism as a topic for discussion by reading Rebecca's comment from her journal that "almost all men were scum and that women deserved every right." Thea declared that she did not support feminist issues. Janet's response was to counter Thea's anti-feminism by articulating a broadly defined human rights position that included race. Janet stated, "I agree with women getting equal pay, rights, but not just for that but also for equalness among races; everyone is equal." She qualified her position by dissociating herself from feminist teachers:

> Well, when a couple of teachers I had, a couple of years ago would say, it's **M s.** because men have Mr. and that doesn't say they're married or not so why do we. I think that's taking it to extremes—like do we really care if you're married or not. . . .When I hear feminism I more or less hear overboard—forgetting all other issues.

The rule concerning feminism was, evidently, not to go "overboard." For Janet who was not afraid to go "overboard" in the violence of her language, the feminist concern with language was seen as trivial. Similarly, she perceived highlighting gender injustices as "extreme." In the quotation above, what seemed to mark feminism as "extreme," as going "overboard," was Janet's concern that other social injustices would be neglected. And she brought other injustices to the fore whenever feminism began to edge its way into the conversation. In the previous quotation Janet deflected attention from feminism by referring to racial oppression: the absence of "equalness among races." In one session I related a comment I had overheard in halls where one young woman had said something to the effect that there was no gender problem in the world today. The response was to draw attention to social class. Zandra, one of the other students in the study, began by commenting on the person who had made the comment:

> Zandra: This person is living in a bubble.
> Helen: But you tell me that you don't think about gender oppression, that you don't feel oppressed in your own lives. Is that right?

Zandra: Yes, but it still happens in other people's lives. You see it but
[She pauses.]
Janet: We just happen to be lucky.
Zandra: Yeah.
Janet: But I think we realize that people struggle. This school for instance, a fair number of these people can't afford to go to university, can't afford a decent meal. A lot of these people come to school and don't have breakfast, don't have lunch and wait until they get home for dinner type of thing. We see this.

It appeared that for Janet the way to prevent going "overboard" was to remind oneself and others of all the other kinds of oppressions there are in the world. The point seemed to be to diminish the collective oppression of women by invoking other injustices.

In a similar vein, Janet indicated during her interview that the study's focus on women's oppression was too narrow:

Janet: I think that maybe we should have read some more stuff besides women—what am I trying to say here. . . .
Helen: It wasn't extreme but— [I pause.]
Janet: Um, it's just, like, women don't get treated equally, and we don't get enough of the same pay, and I think we went on that too long. . . . It was just we had too much of it. Like too many authors doing the same thing. . . . It was just too many poems that were too similar. If every poem would have been about death, then I would have got sick about death too and that happened to be the topic.
Helen: Right, it still could have been about women's experience.
Janet: Yeah, yeah.
Helen: And it still could have had women authors, so that's not the problem. [I pause.]
Janet: We started to hear about men—don't treat us right, they give us rotten wages, I can't get into Canada.. . . men are looking at me funny 'cause I'm a dangerous woman.' Why can't, like, I'm sure these people have written other stuff besides that, that's been really good and really powerful, and it might have been on men and how nice they are.
Helen: Okay.
Janet: Or even about love, or breaking up with a boyfriend. You don't have to say it's not fair, I'm not getting a fair wage.
Helen: Okay, Janet, okay. I think I understand that. Something else beside the oppressive aspects about being a woman.
Janet: Right.

There was a curtness and a woodenness to the way Janet initially responded to the questions. The conversation seemed irritating and/or confusing as she struggled to define what "going overboard," and "being extreme" meant in this study. She concluded that there was some-thing extreme or limited about speaking of women's oppression. Her line that the poetry could have focused "on men and how nice they are" or about "love and breaking up with a boyfriend" suggests that issues important to her were eclipsed or suppressed by a focus on women's oppression. It was not simply a focus on the positive experiences of being a woman that Janet was asking for, since she included the potentially negative experience of "breaking up with a boyfriend." Rather, what seemed to be troubling about feminist avant-garde writing was the uncomfortable possibility of excluding men by failing to see them as "nice" or desirable.

It may have been that heterosexuality was defining for Janet (and for the others) her own gender identity, or at least part of it. Janet and the other young women in this study seemed to define themselves as women based on a notion of heterosexuality: what Deborah Britzman (1993) calls "heteronormativity"—the assumption that women love men.[1] When Janet wrote and spoke of how she and her friend Selena "share[d] men," it may have meant that men were objects or property to be shared among friends. Because men could be "shared," the young women did not need to see each other as competitors, which was important to the maintenance of their friendship. It could also be that Janet was saying that she and her friend liked the same kind of men or, taken more metaphorically, that part of what bound her and Selena together was a shared interest in men. This last possibility suggests that what Janet and the others may have been using to define women as women and bind women together was their shared interest in men.

The study seemed to evoke or create the possibility of a subject position "woman" and more particularly, "young women" outside of a notion of men. For young women claiming heterosexuality, this may have been troubling or, at the very least, uncomfortable to explore. It raised the question how else to define oneself as a young woman.

There were other concerns that the literature evoked. Janet mentioned that she had difficulty relating to the Bronwen Wallace poem "Between Words":

I couldn't relate to it. . . . All I want to say is that they deserve it cause they're stupid and they should know that isn't the only way—that they can get out of it. It doesn't matter where you live and there's a way to get out of it. Come on girls.

Despite acknowledging her own problems with school, Janet had little sympathy for women in the Bronwen Wallace poem. For Janet, their lack of agency was unappealing and unreasonable. To acknowledge that women may be oppressed would seem to put at risk the pleasure and fun of flirting with boys, of "sharing" men, and the pleasure and power in thinking that the world is yours.

What Janet managed to produce in this study were poems about the teacher-student relationship, the parent-child relationship and, in one instance, a poem about her female friends. The students in the poems were not gendered, but it is interesting that the teachers were identified as female. It is "Ms. Smith" that is the focus of the anger and the violence expressed in her poem "The! Devil! the Angel, the teacher and ME." I suspect a female teacher or school librarian's voice and Janet's own voice are represented in her poem "Class." The last section of the poem reads:

> The Book must be returned
>   in two days.
> But I can't read
>   War and Peace
>   that quick.
> Sorry those are the rules
>   Have an apple my sweet.
> And I can't break the rules.
>   The red one's the juiciest.

Janet depicted the teacher/librarian's politeness—the sign of the "good woman"—as a vehicle to disguise the unreasonable use of power and authority. It is this "politeness" that is in stark contrast with Janet's own use of language and demonstrates Janet's rejection of the "good girl." The poem also relies on the expectation that teachers, perhaps female teachers in particular, should be advocates for students.

Janet expressed similar sentiments in her poem "Child of Love," in which the relationship between parent and the child was identified specifically as that of mother and son. The section of the poem where this was most apparent reads:

> Daddy ran away.
> You R the man, now,
> make me dinner
> go to bed, get a life.
> FUCK OFF.
> I don't like your girlfriend
> she's a slut
> Daddy's gone clean youR room
> I WANT DINNER
> It's cold reheat it
>
> good night dear, I love you.

Janet wrote in her journal that this poem concerned "the nasty things parents would or might say that stick in a little kid's head." In both cases the poems are built on an expectation that parents and teachers should be looking after the student or child and are not. The women are positioned in these poems as particularly responsible.

Like Rebecca, Zandra, Denise, and Thea, Janet took advantage of an opportunity to write about female friendships. Unlike the others, she wrote in less than glowing terms about her previous female friends with the exception of the "true best friend" Selena. While this work was women-centered in that Janet focused on her female friends, it was not from a feminist or collective experience that she wrote. Nonetheless, the research project opened up a possibility of writing about female friendships. Perhaps this topic in the context of this study created an opening in which Janet and the others could centre the category of women without invoking feminism or threatening heterosexual desire.

Conclusion

Unlike most of the other students, Janet seemed really to have enjoyed the experience of the study and the poems she wrote and read. Her desire to perform an identity of "rebel" could be easily mapped on to an alternative vision of femininity and of the female writer as rule-breaker offered in feminist avant-garde writing. I suspect for Janet, there was something delicious about breaking rules, particularly school rules. At least that is how I "read" and "write" her with much pleasure of my own. The image transgresses traditional notions of femininity defined in terms of passivity, politeness, compliance, and selflessness. The rebel image seemed to Janet to secure greater agency in satisfying her own interests/desires in the world. On the other hand, Janet's work with feminist avant-garde writing also illuminated boundaries that limited the rules she would break and the writing she would do. In other words, there were investments and commitments that policed or regulated the "rebel" in particular ways that prevented Janet from entertaining notions of "woman" produced in feminist avant-garde writing. Like the other young women in the study, formidable investments in personal agency and heterosexuality constituted barriers that were difficult to write across, even for a rebel.

A Sample of Janet's Poetry

(untitled)

jane we fought we competed
she used me for my pool
she copied my homework and
stole my barbie
she just got too good for me so she thought.

melissa we dressed up in mom's clothes
tried to look sexy flatted chested
three feet tall
didn't want to bleed to become sisters
so we stood on either side of a creek and
held hands then promised to stay friends
forever.

sharena was bigger than me and pushed
me around i liked boys she didn't
hated my boyfriends tried to drown me
in her pool
she just got too good for me or so she thought.

selena talks listens cares shares
double dates shopping trips shared sports
shared men shared dinner
never got too good for me.

Future School for Robots and Humanoids

click, click, click
the gears turn,
click, click, click

wandering door to door
empty smiles or familiar faces
yak, yak goes the robot
at the front of the room

click, click
the gears turn,
click, click
start the cycle over

process the information
categorize, alphabeticalize,
in chronological order,
don't hit the wrong button

click, click, click,
the gears keep turning,
click, click, click
do not pass go, go directly to jail,

to question is the enemy,
the program is to learn
termination is the answer
for a glitched circuit.

The! Devil!, The Angel, the teacher and ME

nag, nag, nag, nag, nag, nag, nag
FUCK OFF BITCH.
nag, nag, nag, nag, nag
Say! It! Out! Loud! Stupid!
nag, nag, nag,
Only a few more days
I WON'T BLOW IT.
nag, nag, nag, nag
AHHHHHHHHHHH
nag, nag, nag,
She! Hasn't! Said! Anything! Useful! Yet!
She's teaching you humility
nag, nag, nag, nag,
ONLY A FEW DAYS LEFT.
!!B——R——I——N——G——!!
nag, nag, nag.
Kill! Her! Stupid!
SEE YOU TOMORROW MS. SMITH.

You graduate next week.

Chapter Six

Threatening the Romantics

Lauren, Denise, and Zandra

This chapter describes the responses of the three other students in the study: Lauren, Denise, and Zandra. For various reasons, these young women produced much less writing than did the others. But, however limited, their responses echo in interesting ways the themes that evident in the responses of Rebecca, Thea, and Janet, and at other times, they offer unique perspectives and articulations. I begin with Lauren who, out of all the students, was the most positive about the study and about feminist avant-garde writing.

Lauren

Like the other students, Lauren was seventeen years old and in her last year of high school. She is white, and I suspect middle-class. At the time of the study, Lauren was relatively new to the school and the area, having previously lived in a number of cities in Europe and in Canada. She did not know the other students in the study. According to Lauren she experienced a great deal of difficulty with her school work due to what she saw as her limited intellectual ability. At one point she said rather lightheartedly, "I am always going to summer school because I'm always failing something." Although Lauren struggled with her school work she liked English class and read and wrote voraciously in her spare time. She had what might be considered an antiquarian interest in books. "I just love books!!" Lauren wrote in her journal, "I own 94 novels, 10 hardcovers, 1 Bibble [sic],

5 dictionnaries [sic] and 2 text books. The Library is so much like heaven. . . . I have a book from 1899, way before there was such a thing as copyright. And I have a Websters [sic] Dictionnary [sic] from 1940." Lauren tended to read popular fiction. During the study she mentioned reading novels by John Updike, Stephen King, and Jackie Collins. Lauren told me that she often read and wrote when feeling bored or depressed.

Lauren seemed extremely comfortable with feminist avant-garde literature and spoke enthusiastically about the class seminars. During her interview she commented. "I liked [the study]. It was very weird, you know, not too many people would do this [kind of work]. And I like English so I really did like this." Although she liked the poetry read during the class seminars, Lauren did not write about or discuss feminism directly nor did she easily or exuberantly use the poetry in the study to inform her own writing. But in comparison with the other students, she seemed less disturbed by the literature and had no difficulty identifying with the characters in it. This may have to do with the very personal responses she had to the literature, her more liberal attitudes towards feminism and poetry, and, I suspect, her less conventional tastes. Lauren would often remark with some enthusiasm that a poem was unusual and for that reason alone she enjoyed it: " I liked it. It was weird." Unlike Janet, Lauren's pleasure in unconventional work did not seem to be related to her attitudes towards schooling and teachers. She simply seemed to enjoy works that broke with convention.

Over the course of the study, Lauren wrote six one-page journal entries, three completed poems totalling 76 lines, and three rough drafts of poems. Her journal entries were curious in that she wrote very personally, using a diary format, despite knowing that I would be reading the entries. For example, her first entry began, "I met Helen Harper, today She is doing research about woman author's [sic] and young girls who write." She finished the entry with a statement that provided some indication of why she decided to participate in the study: "I hope that this group thing will be fun . . . probably more fun than sitting in class and having a certain somebody stare at me for 75 minutes."

Lauren participated in the discussions, although she was not as verbal as the others she seemed actively engaged. Lauren was absent for a number of the seminars which concerned her. She began her second journal entry: "I missed a few days of our sessions and I hope Helen doesn't think I'm not serious about our group; I am, but I've been sick." Because of her illness, Lauren missed some of the poems in the study that students found most provocative, as well as our discussions of feminism. This undoubtedly affected her identification with the literature and her general engagement with the study as a whole.

Pleasure in Poetry: Identifying With Women's Poems

Lauren read a great deal of popular fiction and seemed to enjoy these books immensely. However, her initial attitude towards poetry was less than enthusiastic. In the first session Lauren commented, " I forgot to say that I hate reading poetry. For some reason I can only write but not read poetry." Weeks later she wrote, "maybe reading poems isn't so bad" and later in the same entry, "I used to think reading poetry was boring but all the poems you brought in were interesting to read so I'm inbetween." By "inbetween" I believe she meant she neither hated nor loved poetry. In her second to last entry she told me she had borrowed four books of poetry from the school library and planned to read them. In the next and last entry (dated the following day), she wrote exuberantly, "Last night I was up until 3:00 a.m. reading poetry and my favorite book of poems is called 'The Pill Versus the Springhill Mine Disaster' by Richard Brautigan." Although it was a rather quick conversion from hating poetry to reading it until 3:00 in the morning, Lauren seemed sincere. It is important that the four books of poetry she chose to read were not written by women, nor were they necessarily about women. But in response to the poetry offered in the seminars, Lauren, at least, took up the opportunity to explore the genre.

Lauren expressed a less rigid view about what defines poetry and seemed less resistant to the feminist politics than the other students in the study. This became apparent during her interview when Lauren was commenting on a poem we read in class "I Saw a Monster, " which addressed the topic of male violence against women using strong visual elements. While Thea and Rebecca attempted to distance themselves from this poem, Lauren did not dismiss or deflect the poem's topic but instead seemed personally engaged by the piece:

> Lauren: And this part, the picture, [part of the poem] reminds me of the
> Montreal Massacre and that makes me sick.
> Helen: It was upsetting.
> Lauren: Yeah, because this part—to think of some man killing you—it
> made me sick.

The poem triggered a memory for Lauren of the 1989 murder of
fourteen women in Montreal and she responded personally, imagin-
ing herself in the situation—"to think of some man killing you."
Lauren did not try to deflect the gendered aspect of this kind of
violence, nor did she reject the poem and its topic on the basis of its
politics. Instead Lauren imagined herself as the target of male
violence, adopting, at least for the moment, the subject position of
woman as a victim or target of male aggression. She did this without
invoking concerns about or resistance to a feminist politics or to
avant-garde poetry.

For Lauren the form and content of the poems did not make
suspect subject positions offered in the literature. This became evident
when Lauren commented on the form of one of the poems, indicating
a more open definition of poetry than what was forwarded by the
other students:

> Lauren: Yeah, I liked it [the poem "I saw a Monster"]. People, these
> days wouldn't consider it a poem, some people, you know.
> Helen: What do you think? Is it a poem?
> Lauren: Yeah. And anyways it's like, if rap is or isn't poetry, or if what
> is on greeting cards is or isn't poetry or poet's corner, but I think that
> anything that expresses feeling is a poem, even if its one word or, I
> don't know. . . even though I might not be able to write with different
> forms or play around with it. I guess maybe because I've been warped
> into thinking that's how it is, right, but then that's how I like it too. I
> like a lot of words that fill up the page so I can look at it and be proud
> of myself . . . and it took me time, you know.

Lauren's comment that "anything that expresses feelings is a
poem" served to legitimate the writing studied in the class seminars.
She operated from a position of inclusion rather than exclusion, although Lauren acknowledged that she could not, nor did she wish to,
write poetry that was as innovative as her definition would allow. What

is interesting in this quotation was that, although Lauren knew she had been taught (warped) into believing a particular standard of what poetry was, she admits her pleasure in more conventional poetry (but then I like it too). Evidently her pleasure in writing more conventional poetry did not stop her from reading and accepting the poetry in the study or the subject positions it offered.

Lauren claimed she "learned a lot" from the poetry studied in the seminars. She commented about this learning:

> Helen: Lauren, tell me about what you thought about the whole unit? Was it a good experience?
> Lauren: Yeah, it was, it was. To me a poet— I never really thought as just a man or a girl. I always thought of both, but I never knew there was such poems as these, you know what I mean. To me because maybe I was warped into just poems like a haiku or something, just a couple of lines and they rhyme and talk about flowers, you know. So I learned a lot and I liked it.
> Helen: Did the fact the poets were all women or the feminist stuff, did that bother you?
> Lauren: No it didn't. It was just their way of crying out. Saying how they feel. I can't voice a lot of my emotions. I like to write it down— it's easier for me.

Though she might have been exaggerating, Lauren's comment, "I never knew there were such poems as these [the poems in the study]" indicated that the literature had opened up something new for her. From what she said in the quotation, Lauren seemed to find nothing particularly disconcerting about the feminist focus. Her comment that the poetry was a way for women to express themselves—"it was just their way of crying out. Saying how they feel"—suggests that Lauren can name or mark gender, quite unlike Janet, who adamantly refused this position. Not only did Lauren suggest that women need to "cry out" but she identified with this need quite personally: "I can't voice a lot of my emotions. I like to write them down—it's easier for me."

Lauren engaged with the literature often by comparing it to her own life. This was particularly evident during the interview. As we went through the list of poems that she particularly liked, Lauren described the works repeatedly in terms of what they reminded her of in her own life:

Lauren: I liked "Baglady" because my friend she is a street vendor and in the summer time I go downtown with her . . . and so I know lots of poor people, lots of homeless people. And that would kind of describe a homeless person. . . . Another reason that I like it was, have you ever seen "The Breakfast Club"? It reminds me of that.

Lauren: It's weird—I liked it. It reminds me of *Married with Children* like Peggy Bundy, somehow. . . . "Rhymes to Grow By"—I liked it because it reminds me of when I was little.

Lauren: "Passmore Street" is the same as "Rhymes to Grow By." There's one part when she gets pushed into a pool by her friends. That happened to me a lot.

Helen: And "The Women in this Poem"?
Lauren: Reminds me of my sister. Yeah, because her marriage isn't that good. She wants to leave, but she doesn't have a job and her husband is supporting her and she has her dreams.

For Lauren the poems provided moments to recall events concerning her family, her friends, and her life in general. The poems were relevant to her and as such were perhaps quite unlike the poems she had taken in school—the haiku and the poems that "rhyme and talk about flowers." The situations she named in the last two quotations above concern, among other things, the inability of Lauren and her sister to control circumstances in their lives. The treatment Lauren receives from her friends, and her sister's inability to leave a bad marriage suggest that Lauren has no difficulty in admitting that she and her sister do not always have agency in the world. Again this was quite unlike Janet, who insisted on her own agency. Although Lauren certainly desired agency in her life, I suspect she did not see herself as "lucky" so may have found it easier to work with the subject positions offered in the feminist avant-garde literature.

"She Has Her Dreams": Agency and Heterosexuality

The literature studied in the class seminars functioned as cues for Lauren to talk about her family and friends in class, during her interview, and in her journal. In all but one journal entry, she wrote about personal relationships with her family or friends. More than anything else, Lauren used her journal entries as a personal diary to discuss heterosexual relationships. These relationships were obviously very important to her and served to define "teenage girl" for her. Lauren wrote, "I was really upset. I don't know why, probably over a guy, as usual. . . ." and later, "Don't worry Helen, I'm not sexually obsessed I'm just a teenage girl."

I suspect she struggled with female sexuality and its naming. For example, at one point she wrote: "I'm most definitely no hose-bag [slut], far from it. I just admire men . . . escially [sic] tall dark masculine men with sexy voices. All of the above are tall, dark, mascule [sic] and have sexy voices, except for Peter he has beautiful long red hair and hazel eyes." Often her comments about men were idealized, but the poetry in the seminars did not offer her much in terms of idealized romantic male-female relationships. Indeed men were rarely mentioned in any of the poems, and when they were it was not in terms of heterosexual desire.

This comment about her relationship with men was characteristic of Lauren throughout the study. For her and for Janet, the study seemed to allow an opportunity to discuss their relationships with men and about sexuality in particular. For Janet the avant-garde literature supported constructs of the so-called "bad girl" and the "rebel" that provided grounds for her to transgress traditional sanctions against discussions of sexuality and "flirting with men." It seemed to me there was a sense of fantasy to Lauren's writing. She, perhaps like many teenagers, idealized aspects of romantic heterosexual relationships.

In the first session I described the study to the students and also explained that they would be identified by pseudonyms. While all the students seem really interested in "renaming themselves," Lauren seemed to be particularly excited by this possibility. She chose to comment about it in her first journal entry, "Everything we say, do or write will be an anymous [sic] to our names. I hope my name will be Lorna [later changed to Lauren]. That's the name I use when I pick up men, especially men who bug me with lines like "What's cookin', good lookin" or "hey beautiful, what's your name?" In her next entry she wrote, "I use them [fake names] so I feel *I'm in control . . . 'I know something you don't know'* . . . and chances are I'll never see these men again, so why not?" Changing her name, Lauren seemed to gain control over circumstances in her life, or at least over the men to whom she felt contempt.

Another time when Lauren spoke of agency and control came when she spoke about the poem "I Fight Back" by Lillian Allen:

> Lauren: I can't voice a lot of my emotions. I like to write it down—it's easier for me, or talk on the phone. I can't do it straight out. Some people are really good at that, like my sister. Both my sisters are good at telling people off. I wish I was.
> Helen: Well, everyone has their own way.
> Lauren: Oh that "I Fight Back" I like that one. It reminds me of a big, fat, black woman, Rasta, with long dreads in a fishnet. Just for some reason, I can just imagine a lady like that sitting down on her porch writing. Some images are good.

The Rasta woman image, and her real-life sisters, provided an example of strong women that Lauren found particularly admirable. The feminist literature seemed to provide Lauren an opportunity to imagine the category "woman" outside of notions of passivity and subordination. And she had a strong desire to be more assertive, more powerful in the world—"I wish I was [like that]."

Lauren patterned three poems after several poems studied in class. According to Lauren the form and idea for her first poem "Sweet Lauren" (which appears in its entirety at the end of this chapter) came from the poem "Stairwell Home" [inaccurately referred to as "The Baglady"] and, in terms of the theme, from her recent reading of a Jackie Collins' novel. Her poem "Confusion" was written in the block form of "the hairdresser," and her last poem "Money" used multiple-narrative voices patterned after two poems studied in study: "Sight" and "so i'm afraid of getting what i want?" With the exception of "Sweet Lauren," Lauren's poems did not directly address women's experiences. Lauren's poems are more like Thea's in terms of theme and style. Her poems are narrated by a nebulous " I " unmarked by gender or class, who comments about a general theme. Lauren's poem "Confused" is typical. A section of it reads:

> But I have a question. . . . Has anyone ever figured out the meaning of life? Figured out what that feeling is that we get when we really want and dream about something?

Lauren participated in this study enthusiastically. She seemed to enjoy reading literature that broke with convention. Although she named such work as "weird," Lauren saw the work as worthy and legitimate. Nonetheless, she considered her own writing as quite conventional. Lauren understood writing and reading to be very personal practices. She depicted and produced writing as a form of emotional release, as a place to fantasise and to comment about life. She, like the other students, inserted heterosexual desire into seminar discussions. But more than the other students, she seemed to identify quite easily with the literature.

Denise

Denise, another white seventeen-year-old student, was a close friend of both Rebecca and Zandra. The three of them sat together during the seminars, spoke and worked together, and referred to each other in their comments to the group. The three of them shared a strong interest in science fiction, and in creative writing generally. Like many of the other students in the study Denise wrote for fun in her spare time. She also kept a diary. She shared her writing with her friends and sometimes her family, although she said her mother did not necessarily understand her writing and hated science fiction. Denise liked to read everything but romance which she described as "stupid, [and] very fake." When asked about science fiction, she insisted it needed to be "believable" in order for her to enjoy it. Denise had attempted to write some science fiction prior to the study and was thrilled about what she had produced. She wrote in her first journal entry, "I have just recently made an attempt at science fiction writing. For my first effort I think it's rather good. . . . actually it's great. Perhaps I should be modest, but I become excited when I realize my latest effort at writing is so catchy." Like Rebecca, Denise was highly invested in the identity of "writer" and planned to enter a community college writing program once she graduated.

Denise commented that the topics for school writing assignments were frequently not interesting but "you have to do it." She contrasted school writing with her personal writing: "When you're at home you can make it as long as you want. It's like **your** feelings and thoughts, **your** point of view." Denise greatly enjoyed this sense of freedom in her own personal writing. When Rebecca mentioned that in creative writing classes, "you're trying to please everyone—so everyone will like it" and then added that a school essay was similar, Denise interjected quickly, "An essay is for a teacher, a story is to please me." During her interview Denise stated "I love writing, but I don't like it if you HAVE to write." For Denise creative writing was a space in which she was or should be free to follow her own interests and inclinations outside of the critical gaze of the teacher. In her creative writing class she appreciated what she saw as the freedom to "write what you want" in the class.

During her interview she described the experience of the study, saying, "It was good but I don't know, I didn't get totally wrapped up in it." And she really did not get "wrapped up" in it. Despite Denise's enthusiasm for creative writing, the literature did not seem to inspire her. Indeed she seemed increasingly frustrated by the study as a whole, and with me in particular. At one point in her interview she told me, "like, I can write, you know; but I don't write every week. Every time I see you, it's like 'I'm not that creative, you've killed my creative juices. I can't think anymore'."

Evidently, from what Denise wrote in her first journal entry, she had had little difficulty in coming up with topics in the past. She wrote:

> I believe it was Thea who said that she found it difficult to think of a topic. I found that rather strange because I don't "think" of topics to write about. When I begin a story I usually write a line or even a few words and I'm off. I don't have to think about what I'm writing, it just comes.

During her interview she spoke of how students would ask her for ideas for their creative writing assignments. Apparently after the study Denise did not experience difficulty generating ideas or energy for her writing. During the interview I asked her about this:

Helen: Are you still writing? Everything is fine that way?
Denise: Yeah, I'm writing for English a forty or fifty page thing for the term.
Helen: Forty or fifty pages!
Denise: Yeah, I'm doing like an anthology: three stories.

Yet during this study Denise's energy and enthusiasm seemed to diminish. She did produce four journal entries, three poems, and a short story. The poems totalled 63 lines and the short story was six pages long. There were a number of drafts begun but never submitted. Denise attended all the sessions and seemed engaged in the discussion and in the readings. Although not a frequent contributor, Denise offered occasional comments. She also shared writing she had done previously and shared a favourite poem. However, distress and frustration mounted as the study progressed. Like Thea, Denise stopped submitting journal entries about halfway through the study. Her last journal entry was only half a page long and began by indicating she was experiencing difficulties. She wrote: "The problems I've had with my writing, well, I am too tired to write anything much for you. I did start a detective story starring Dixon Hill, a character on the holodeck, from the 1940s that Captain Picard loves to play, but, I've been busy with other work and I never had time to continue it."

Killing Creative Juices

In the final interview Denise attributed her frustration during the study to the increasing demands of her school work. I asked her what I should do differently if I was to run the study again and she replied:

> Don't make it so long. . . . Everything is fine now but at the time I was hoping the earth would swallow me. I had so much stuff, I couldn't think straight. I was stressed out. . . . I guess some people don't take stress well. I went just "Leave me alone. Get out of my way. Don't ask me anything. Let me get this done." I'm not that organized. I never give myself enough time so I kind of did myself in.

No doubt some of the difficulty Denise experienced in the study had to do with the demands of her school work. Certainly it is difficult to be creatively inspired when one is exhausted, and it is easy to become irritable when one is feeling the pressure of deadlines. It is interesting and important that Denise spoke of the desire to be left alone—not to be asked "anything." There is a sense of wishing to escape the intrusiveness of others and their demands. This study was intrusive for Denise, but it was not simply a matter of time constraints.

There did seem to be a kind of "killing" of her creative juices, a dampening of her energy. It is possible that the questions and assignments were asking more of her than she could or wanted to do. Although it seems contradictory, Denise's desire to be free from the constraints in her writing made the study, which sought to break the constraints of form on writing, more difficult. She was not comfortable with the premises, pleasures, and practices of feminist avant-garde writing. Whereas for Janet the feminist literature opened up possibilities, for Denise it seemed to close down opportunities.

Part of the intrusiveness of the study that seemed to inhibit Denise concerned her sense of obligation to me personally. Denise indicated several times that she wrote mainly out of an obligation she felt towards me. In her journal entry, Denise writes, "I am too tired to write anything much for you." In claiming she was writing for me, and not in her own interest, Denise could distance herself from her writing and from the literature. The study could be defined as simply schoolwork done to please the teacher or, in this case, the researcher. During the interview she told me that she could not use the poems in the study but felt she had to produce something so that she would not offend me:

> Helen: This one [pointing to a poem of Denise's] I remember this one you said came from listening to the radio and the last two [poems] from other personal experiences but your inspiration didn't ever come from the poems we studied.
> Denise: I thought I've GOT to do something for her [Helen] or she'll think I'm totally ignoring her. . . . I used the formats and stuff. But I guess, I don't know, I just couldn't take it from that I was like, I don't relate kind of.
> Helen: That's really interesting Denise. If you could tell me a little more about that.
> Denise: I don't know. I just— "Fear" [one of the poems taken in class] I thought, it's great. I'm glad they can write like that but I don't think I can. It's great. I appreciate it but I don't think the next time I write I'll try something like that. Maybe, I would try it, but it isn't really my style. I kind of write—I don't know how I write—I just write.

Denise seemed quite interested in the poems during the sessions. However, her writing was motivated by an obligation to me and her strong desire to be a "good girl" or a "good student" put additional pressure on Denise. My efforts and my concern to draw her out was all the more an irritant. The more interest I showed Denise, the more pressure she was under to produce and to negotiate with feminist avant-garde writing, which was difficult since it was not "her style." The advantage to claiming that one is not personally invested in the writing is that difficulties in the writing can be relocated in the teacher or in the assignment. She can say the teacher "killed her creative juices." Denise does in one instance relocate the problem as existing in her own personality and her resistance to change:

> Helen: So [the literature] never connected with you?
> Denise: Maybe I'm too set in my ways. "This isn't going to change me. I'm just going to keep writing this way." I guess, I tried—I tried too, like in "Into the Darkness."
> Helen: There was a change in the lines here [pointing to a verse]. There seemed some sort of conscious effort—
> Denise: Actually I don't think that was from the stuff you gave us. It was just to make the person slow down for dramatic effect. It was a subconscious effort. It has to go like that, just because, it just does.

It could be that Denise was just "too set in her ways," but the question is why this was so. What intellectual and affective investments were displaced by the literature, and the project, and evidently, by me? During the interview I asked her about the feminist perspective offered in the literature and whether that had interfered with her ability to relate to the materials. Like the other students, she carefully located herself outside a feminist identity:

> Helen: Anything else that strikes you about the class, anything we talked about—Did the feminist stuff offend you in any way?
> Denise: I don't remember. I think I just read it and went, 'that's fine, that's their opinion.' I think feminists get carried away at points. Everything offends them.
> Helen: So that wasn't an interfering factor or anything?
> Denise: No, no, not really. 'Mankind', why isn't it 'womenkind', and I'm like it's just general.
> Helen: Did it bother you that there were only women poets in the readings?
> Denise: No I thought it was great. I'm glad they're writing stuff and getting recognized. That's great. Finally women are writing.

Evidently the feminist content was not an interfering factor, but it clearly did not evoke her interest, nor was there any sense of her own investment in the statement "Finally women are writing." What was identified most strongly as an "interfering factor" in this study, what was an unwelcomed and unwanted intrusion, were the questions, the analysis, the criticisms (positive and negative) about her writing and about the literature in the study. Denise latched onto the notion of analysing as an intrusive factor for her:

> Helen: So when you think of the whole project—Is there anything that sticks out in your mind. Things you still think about or thought about then, or anything that stuck with you.
> Denise: I don't know, it seemed to take forever. I got tired of it after a while. No offence, but, it was "Oh God, she's coming again—How much more analysing can I do?"

Later in the same interview we spoke further about this:

> Denise: Don't analyse so much. . . .well, like analyse it a smidge, but don't go 'why this, why that?" It's like, oh God, you can't just take it at face value or just say little things, a little bit of analysing but not like every little thing. I don't sit there and say "why did they write it like that, and what were they thinking."
> Helen: or how might this relate to my own life?
> Denise: I don't do that. It drives me crazy.

Analysing Desire

For Denise the problem with analysing came up in two specific instances during the study. At one point she brought in a poem to share with the others, as I had suggested they might do. It was a love poem found in a daily newspaper. Denise read the poem aloud and then the group discussed it. The students expressed their approval. I asked Denise about what she liked about the poem.

> Denise: It's beautiful. It's a man, his expression of his love, you know. It's beautiful. It's a metaphor for their love. She's the ocean and he's the light and they come together and they fit so perfectly.

Helen: Wow. [reading the poem] "When you reflect my burning love within I become whole." It is beautiful, but there's something that bothers me here—"when you reflect my burning love I become whole."
Denise: He's not complete without her.
Helen: The only thing is that, it's from his perspective and it's beautiful, it breaks your heart but, on the other hand, what about her [the woman in the poem]? What is she getting out of this? This one line I love its sweetness, but—
Denise: This is just one man's view. If you want her view, go search her out.
Helen: Why doesn't he say I hope you too are made whole?
Denise: Do you have to pick apart everything?
Helen: It's a question for me of what love is about—mutuality.
Denise: It's just—he's expressing his love to this woman.
Helen: How he chooses to express his love is important.
Denise: It's beautiful.
Helen: Yes, it is beautiful but if I said that the reason why I love you is because I see myself reflected in you—
Zandra: That's just one of the reasons.
Denise: He's just saying when you reflect my love—He's the light.
Helen: [laughing] Oh yeah, he's the light and she's the mirror and of course this is what women are supposed to be all the time, mirrors exaggerating men's image of themselves back to themselves.
Denise: NO. You're taking it out of context. Who cares? Just take it from what's there.
Helen: Just let it wash over you? But his view, this has serious consequences.
Denise: So you can dump him and I'll take him because he's extremely sweet.
Helen: It's sweet to write a poem.
Denise: It's just a poem, okay. It's just a poem. Something spontaneously written—
Rebecca: Well he had to make it rhyme, maybe he just needed a line to rhyme—
Janet: Actually this just makes me think of a poem I have in my mind.

Conversation then turned to Janet's poem. Although it reads more seriously in print, the tone of the discussion was quite lighthearted. Denise was smiling and laughing, at least until the last line when clearly she was becoming agitated. Evidently for Denise it was acceptable to identify a metaphor in the poem; it was not so acceptable or indeed even impolite to suggest an alternative reading that might dampen one's appreciation of the poem. Analysis of the line was particularly troubling to the students because it disrupted the subject position of women as the object of a man's love. I attempted to acknowledge the pleasure for women and for Denise in this traditional subject position by repeatedly calling the poem "beautiful," but at the same time questioning the subject position and the reading. Clearly Denise would not tolerate such a reading. Despite her claims to the contrary, she was highly invested in this poem and in the subject position available in the poem. In retrospect, rather than offering a counterreading, what was required here was a discussion of the various implications and pleasures inherent in the representation of women as the object of men's love.

However, even had the discussion been more sensitively handled, I suspect Denise would have experienced some difficulty. In all likelihood, the questions and discussion would have served only to diminish her pleasure. It is not surprising that she did not want to "analyse" the poetry in the study, including her own:

> Helen: So when you look through [your] poems, what do you think? Which one do you like?
> Denise: I don't know. I don't really choose the best poem. I just, kind of write my stuff and go "Fine, now it's written." I don't go—I don't really analyse it.

I suspect that Denise wanted most to control the reading and the criticism her work might engender. Denise did not want a close reading; more specifically, she did not want a feminist reading of text. Considering the effect of the analysis, I do not blame her. Within the practices, premises, and pleasures of feminist avant-garde literary formation, it is impossible or difficult to affirm more traditional gender positions and the affective and intellectual investments that underlie them.

Denise did produce some writing for this study. Although she did not use the poetry to inform her own writing, she made attempts to be innovative in the line and verse format of the work she submitted, but in ways different from the innovations offered in the works studied in the seminars. Denise indicated that she found thematic inspiration from events at home rather than from the poetry studied. Her short story was a version of story line from "Star Trek." One of her poems

("Into the Darkness") sounded much like Rebecca's and Thea's, in which there was a sense of personal turmoil, but the "I" of the poem and the cause of the turmoil was not identified. Her last poem ("The Looking Glass") concerned memories of her grandmother's house. The poem was written after we had studied poems on female friendships and one on the death of a woman's aged mother, and this may have had an effect on her choice of topic. Possibly that these poems made available an avenue for Denise to write about her grandmother.

Although Denise did submit writing, the study was a struggle for her. She was determined to retain her "own style," and her identity as a "successful writer" against the alternative understanding of writing (and writer) offered in feminist avant-garde writing. This identity and her pleasure in traditional heterosexual desire was placed at risk in the premises and practices offered in feminist writing, so it was not at all surprising that she negotiated against what it would offer. Considering these investments, her response (to claim that I was the problem and/or that she was the problem, to distance herself from feminism, to distance herself from analysis, and to dismiss the value of literature) was not unexpected. It was extremely difficult for her to connect or identify with feminist avant-garde writing.

Zandra

Zandra is of South East Asian background. At the time of the study she was seventeen years old and was a close friend of Rebecca and Denise's. The three shared similar interests in creative writing and in science fiction. Zandra indicated in the first session that she liked to read "mystery, romance, anything" and that she preferred writing short stories—"very weird ones."

Zandra expressed a great deal of dissatisfaction with the writing she had to complete for her English class and for her creative writing class. In her first and only journal entry, she wrote, "The writing I produce for my English class means nothing to me. There is nothing I get from it (other than the marks!) . . . . The writing I produce for Mr. C. [her creative writing teacher] is unsatisfactory to me. It's filled with great ideas that haven't been explored to the limit because of the [lack of] time that's given to come up with a finished product." Like Denise and Rebecca, Zandra wrote creatively as a hobby and it was enormously important to her: "It means everything." She wrote, "My first serious piece [of writing] was called 'Lazarus Cult!' It was about teenagers in an adventure involving the CIA and a terrorist group. To me it was more important than anything. I just went on a crazy writing spree after that. I tried to write a couple of romances, then I tried a comedy with terror in it." She clearly distinguished between school and personal writing. This separation was evident even in her word choice in the quotations cited above, for while she "writes" for herself, she "produces" a "product" for school.

According to Zandra she liked to write "weird stories." When I asked in what way the stories were "weird," she laughed and said "they were unexpected—real people doing the unexpected." My interest seemed to prompt her to then say that she liked to try new things but "not share with people, with my friends not my teacher. Mr. C. says I should let go but I don't know." Considering the psychological discourse that seemed to dominate her creative writing class, I suspect that her teacher was suggesting that Zandra be less cautious in her writing, that she abandon herself to her writing, something evidently Zandra would not do easily.

Considering how Zandra liked to write "weird," that is, to break with what was expected, this study would seem to be ideally suited for her, but as the work progressed, it was apparent that Zandra's enthusiasm for the literature was quite limited. She did attend all the sessions and she submitted some writing, but she did not seem particularly interested. She submitted only one journal entry and needed coaxing to do that. When I asked her about this in the interview her opinions about the study were made abundantly clear:

Helen: Okay, this is what I have here. Many poems and one journal entry [showing her]. Now did I miss something here?
Zandra: I'm pretty sure I gave you more than one journal entry.
Helen: Is it in your locker?
Zandra: No, it's at home.
Helen: Okay, check at home and if you find it put it in an envelope. Here's my address [writing it down]. Okay. Here are your poems.
Zandra: I can't believe you are actually seriously doing research on this. I mean couldn't you just sort of wing it.

Despite the fact that I had discussed the importance of the study several times during class, Zandra remained unconvinced. For her the research was not something to be taken seriously. Her continued presence may have been simply because her close friends Denise and Rebecca were attending.

Oppression: "It Happens in Other People's Lives"

Zandra strongly resisted the notion of gender oppression in her own life. She was often highly dismissive of feminism. After a session in which Bronwen Wallace's "The Woman in This Poem" was read and discussed, Zandra came to me at the end of the seminar, as I was packing up my papers and, unfortunately, the tape recorder, to tell me that she did not feel as restrained in her life as the women in the poem did. Outside of the interview it was the only time she spoke to me privately. The Wallace poem is interesting in that it forges a connection between the constraints in the life of the female character and the female readers of the poem. Zandra felt strongly enough or uncomfortable enough about this connection to tell me she rejected it. Instead she wanted to insist upon her agency in the world. We spoke about the Bronwen Wallace poem during the interview and she affirmed repeatedly the freedom she felt in her life and her general lack of sympathy for the character:

Helen: Do you remember the poem, "The Women in This Poem." Do you remember, the lover calls and she feels trapped by her kids and husband.
Zandra: If she felt that strongly about it, she should have left her husband and gone to her lover.
Helen: I remember you saying that your life wasn't that constrained the way that woman's life was.
Zandra: I really can't relate to that. Well sometimes I suppose.
Helen: Sometimes?
Zandra: No, not really. . . . If she didn't want it, she shouldn't have done it. That's the way I see it. I mean if she couldn't handle it then she shouldn't have gotten married and whatever, and now if she can't handle it, she should bail out [she pauses]. For her it's personal and for me it's just something that's there. I see it from the outside and it doesn't make much difference to me. But I can't see myself being trapped like that. I can't.

Zandra took an optimistic position that countered the assumption of gender oppression underpinning feminist avant-garde writing. She referred to age as a factor in experiencing oppression or a lack of control over one's—"everyone has felt trapped once or twice in their life, maybe when they were younger." This suggests a definition of adulthood in terms of agency.

In later sessions Zandra admitted that there was oppression in the world, but it "happens in other people's lives." She made a similar comment about a poem by Lillian Allen concerning the experience of Black immigrant women in Canada. Zandra stated that while she herself did not have experience of racial discrimination, she definitely knew "people who did." Much like Janet, Zandra admitted that race and gender oppression does exist in the world but not in her own life. Later in the same seminar she stated that gender was simply not an issue for her and indeed she trivialized it:

> Zandra: I find a lot of these girls talking about feminist stuff. It's weird. I don't know about other people, but I don't write about that. I don't think about it.
> Helen: Yeah. Does anything make you think of it?
> Zandra: Only when my sister and I have to do the dishes, and my brother has to take the garbage out. Why don't I? Not that I want to take the garbage out, but I mean I have to do the dishes, and he just has to take the garbage out.
> Lauren: 'Cause boys are stupid.
> Zandra: That's what my mum says: That boys are too stupid to do the dishes. But only then.
> Helen: Do your parents have other different or higher expectations for you as compared to your brother?
> Zandra: It's an age thing.

Zandra's response to feminist avant-garde writing and its premise of women's oppression was to insist on her own agency and power in the world. She deflected attention in this case from gender to age.

Despite Zandra's beliefs about feminism and about the study, she submitted ten short poems. The majority of these were submitted at the very end of the study. The poems were remarkable in that she first admitted that she didn't like writing poems but in the end submitted more poems than anyone else, although they are short (in total only twelve lines each) and appear to be hastily written. Two of the poems twelve lines each) and appear to be hastily written. Two of the poems address her notion of writing and its value to her. Our discussions in the first seminar about writing may have suggested the topic. She indicated during class that she hadn't used any technique: (it wasn't appealing to me) and that the idea was her own (The idea came to my head when I was doing the dishes. There was no intention to rhyme but some lines do). In her poem her writing is described as her child.

> You are my only child to whip into shape
> You're my only child to mould and to raise
> You're the only child who I will need and praise
> When all the others leave you will
> still be my child.
> You who are my child shall live on forever.

In another poem she described writing as a tool:

> Writing is a utensil, writing is a tool
> Writing is a mechanizism [sic] that
> elevates the soul.
> It's a great giver of strength
> It's more than just the beginning
> It's more than just the end.
> It's the beginning of understanding
> It's the end of my pain
> It's the keystone to my universe
> and everything within.

Zandra, like the other students in the study, depicted writing as a personal and psychological act, and like a child, something under her control. Her poetry was highly personalised, abstract, and, predictably, difficult to share. Several times during the study Zandra mentioned that writing was too personal to share. Her poetry remained abstract, even when she wrote about herself as in her poem "Me":

> I'm the soul without a home
> The rain without water
> I'm the tears that never shall be
> shed
> The child that shall never be loved
> I'm hollow and empty.

Like several of the other students, Zandra wrote about the loneliness, emptiness, and hollowness of a self disconnected from everything, including class, race, and gender identity. Zandra also excluded other affiliations she could have chosen: family, school, friends. The alienation and loneliness expressed in the poems of the teenaged women in my study may, in part, be the inevitable consequence of working within a progressive writing tradition defined within the paradigm of liberal humanism. In this, I am not denying the anguish of the individual, but I am suggesting that the experience is framed within a discourse that disconnects the self and the anguish from its social context. The production of a self that transcends social and historical context means writing that is focused on the exploration of a fixed, stable, unique, and, inevitably solitary soul. The shift to political and social marking becomes largely unnecessary and unwelcomed. This was quite different from what is required in feminist avant-garde writing. As evident throughout the data, the students largely negotiated against any gender or race affiliation offered in feminist avant-garde writing.

Zandra also ignored the opportunities for experimentation with literary form and language convention, with one notable exception. Her last and I believe her best poem concerned her sister, written after we had studied a poem that featured sisters as characters. Zandra's poem "Our Bedroom Closet" was interesting in its theme and form, mimicking the poem read in class. While she did not directly refer to gender or race in her work, Zandra could take up the topic of sisterhood and at least attempt to break with traditional form. Like Rebecca, Thea, Janet, and Denise, Zandra also worked on a poem about a female friendship, although in the end she did not submit it. As I've discussed in previous chapters, I believe that writing about sisters or female friends allowed the students to center the category of woman without threatening heterosexuality or invoking women's oppression. Thus the students could avoid a feminist identity. I also rather doubt that these relationships, which are obviously important in their lives, are often available as topics to write about in their English or creative writing class.

As stated previously, Zandra submitted a large number of poems at the very end of the study. Part of the reason she submitted her writing finally may have come from her desire to follow the rules: to be someone who is a "good girl" or "good student," despite the fact that she did not find the study particularly important or relevant.

fact that she did not find the study particularly important or relevant. The notion of "a good girl" was evoked during her final interview in relation to Joy Harjo's poem: "I am a Dangerous Woman":

> Helen: So tell me about "I'm a Dangerous Woman." What did you like about it? Do you think you are a dangerous woman?
> Zandra: No.
> Helen: [laughs] Would you like to be a dangerous woman?
> Zandra: Sure, why not. Everybody wants to. Because I'm supposed to be the goody-goody. My sister is the wild one. . . . She's rebellious even at this stage, but I'm like—I'll do what I'm told, it's okay, I'll do it, kind of thing.

A Desire to Be Dangerous

Although Zandra wished to be a "dangerous woman" one who would rebel against the rules, and she was "suppose to be the goody-goody," earlier in the study she suggested something else:

> Helen: You liked that one [I am a Dangerous Woman]. Tell me why you liked it.
> Zandra: I don't know. I find that some parts of it are true.
> Helen: Are true? Which part?
> Zandra: Her brain, not her body, is dangerous. I think that people don't believe it or buy it but that is, like, a real weapon. I don't know, everyone has a wee bit of that in them.
> Helen: A wee bit of?
> Zandra: I've always been interested in the FBI, CIA, and stuff like that and usually they use women as decoys but to actually think they could do more that just that. I like that—strange. I really like the idea. . . . A lot of people think "she wouldn't go hurt anyone, she wouldn't do anything," but I could. [she laughs]

Here Zandra was able to see herself as possibly breaking expectations: as playing with the possibilities of being dangerous. Clearly she wanted an alternative subject position to the 'good girl' image, "the goody-goody" and the "decoys." Clearly she wanted to be dangerous in the way a man can be dangerous, physically as well as intellectually. Her belief she could be dangerous, that is, Zandra's belief in her own agency made it difficult, if not impossible, to identify with the characters and subject positions offered in the literature since the "woman" in feminist avant-garde writing is marked by gender oppression and by a struggle for agency within the historical context of women fighting for social change. Thus, Zandra, like Denise and to a certain degree like Lauren, ultimately negotiated against the premises, practices, and pleasures of feminist avant-garde literature. Identification with the feminist literature in the project proved difficult for her.

A Sample of Lauren's Poetry

Sweet Lauren

a socialite
calm, cool, beautiful
on
the
outside
sleeping pills, alcohol,
valiums
diet pills
sparkling diamonds, silk
champagne
tummy tucks
size eight
$5,000 dresses
$1,000,000 dollar/plate dinners
lonely, sad
depressed
lost her virginity in the backseat
of a
Limo
on
a
mink coat
she
was
the only person
who
knew, cared
that
she was
fake.

A Sample of Denise's Poetry

The Looking Glass

There it sits against the attic wall, covered by
a faded sheet.
Remove the sheet, brush away the years of dust
          What do you see?
A face, your face, distorted by the shadows
that penetrate the room, with its faded photographs
     and broken trunks,
     Pieces of the past, a puzzle to be solved.
Do you remember where you first saw it?
               Think. Go Back.
Grandmother's house with its lumpy furniture
and sweet smells. It was in her room then.
     Her Room! knitting needles, pearls, perfume,
  You were so small then.
               Innocent
You run your fingers along its frame,
Feel the smoothness, you shiver but the
attic is warm.
               Memories
Put the sheet back on, allow the dust to
collect once more.
The floor creaks as you leave. The dust settles
Lock the door, hold in the memories.

A Sample of Zandra's Poetry

(untitled)

the bathroom door
squeaks and moans and
the door would
tremble at the force
tremble at the force,

and my sister would watch me begin to cry and try to
Pretend
like a broken Barbie
doll
Pretend
I'm the older
but she never CRADLED ME!
Ha!
Ha!

on the twin bed
whissspering a short prayer
into my open diary

Innocent eyes, amused
eyes observed me from
the door
helpstopherhelpstopherhelpstopher

help
stop
her.

Chapter Seven

Dangerous Desires: Disturbing Identifications[1]

Writing can be dangerous. When you are expected to belong in a home that is acceptable, socially or politically or religiously, but you don't, and you write beyond it—it can be very dangerous. . . . the risk was literally feeling that I was going to lose myself, my direction, everything, that I'd go off the edge of the page, the world.
—Betsy Warland in Williamson, 1993

Was I the "good girl" feminist in all of this? Too loyal, too willing to follow "the rules" of feminist avant-garde, or too afraid to take them to their limit, unable to allow/entertain the ambivalence, the ambiguity, the multiplicities, the contradictions of such work?
—My Research Journal

Forget it. I've lost myself now. I don't even know what I'm trying to say.
—Rebecca

Over the course of twelve class sessions the young women in this study generated a great deal of text in their creative writing and journal entries. They participated actively and often enthusiastically in the seminar discussions. Several shared favorite literature and other materials from their personal and school reading. They had a range of responses to the study, to the literary works, and to the creative writing they produced, and all engaged the work at least initially. All the students attempted, in at least some of their work, to use the literature from the study to inform their own creative writing. However, their participation and production belies the fact that the study required difficult and unsettling negotiations with the practices, and premises of feminist avant-garde literature, more specifically with the identity of woman constituted in the literature. This "woman" was not easily or exuberantly adopted by the young women in the study. The literature did not provide them with an easy vehicle for identification.

As described in the preceding chapters, the young women in this study experienced considerable distress with the material. As the study progressed, most of the participants spoke of being tired, irritated, and rather uninspired. Several indicated that they were experiencing difficulty in their writing. There were moments of confusion, hesitation, and anger. For example, Rebecca, in the midst of describing the difference between stories and poems, wrote, "Forget it. I've lost myself now. I don't even know what I'm trying to say." In her interview she commented on one of the poems, "I don't like it and I do like it. It's creative but I don't know if I can really think of it as a poem." And there were instances when students attempted to distance themselves from the project or dismiss it entirely. Zandra, for example, says at one point, "I can't believe you're taking this study seriously." Thea, who left the study early, stated that she preferred to stay in her creative writing class because "we were getting marks on that and not this." Yet they also said that their experience was "basically positive," that they liked the opportunity to read "something weird." But in general the students found the study far more difficult than I had imagined they would, and by the end I suspect they were quite glad to be finished with it.

The reaction of a number of teachers, graduate students, and researchers to the study has been to explain or explain away the students' distress or resistance to the feminist literature by referring to the historical or social contexts in which this study was conducted (a time of feminist backlash); to the research process (the study was not long enough to get to know the students or to see shifts); to developmental and essentialized notions of teenagers (female students at the height of their power in patriarchal society and so less likely to challenge this power; that they are, after all, "teenagers" and "all" teenagers are resistant; that these students hadn't had enough life experience). More frequently there have been critiques of the pedagogy (the pedagogy was too impositional; pedagogical expectations were too high); and of the avant-garde literature itself (the unconventional nature of the work was off-putting). More recently, a female graduate student suggested that my marital status was a factor, and, that as a married woman and a feminist, she would be in a better position to offer the students an example of someone who had negotiated (successfully because of her marital status?) hetero-sexuality and feminism.[2]

Some of these factors do need to be considered in order to produce pedagogical encounters that will ensure that feminism remains to some degree speakable. However, these factors are not the primary focus of this study. Instead, I believe that these factors are a backdrop to the emotional and intellectual commitments or invest-ments that secure particular identities and identifications that young women struggle with in an encounter with feminist avant-garde writing. I suspect the students' commitments or investments may have been less discernible, but present nonetheless, had circumstances been somewhat different. I do not deny the effects of the research context, the specific literary works selected, or pedagogical strategies on the "availability" of alternative discourses and their possible subject positions. But I am assuming that there are consistent emotional and intellectual investments, what Judith Robertson (1994) refers to as "forcelines," that would need to be negotiated regardless of the specific circumstances. Better, more sensitive pedagogy, for example, might have made the negotiations less dramatic, the experience less volatile, but negotiations would still have occurred, as they would with exposure to any new literary or discursive formation. More effective feminist pedagogy will depend on understanding what is at stake for young women in their renderings of themselves, and how their affective and intellectual investments are produced. Only then can we learn to work with and/or against these investments. This has been expressed by some academics as working with resistance (Pitt, 1996; Bogdan, 1994; Wolff, 1991).

The students' views about feminism, literature, creative writing and the construct of "good girl student" seemed to hold together as highly invested identities that the feminist avant-garde literature threatened. This chapter will review briefly and then discuss in greater depth the themes apparent in the data and conclude with the implica-tions of these findings with regard to identification and identity formation, and the promise of feminist avant-garde literature as a pedagogical resource for feminist teachers and their students.

The Danger of Feminism: Risking Heterosexuality and Agency

As evident in the data chapters, the strongest sanction against identifying with the literature was its feminist focus. Although the participants were aware of the nature of the study and the kind of literature they would be reading, the young women read the work as radically feminist, and feminism, as they understood it, was simply unpalatable. The study was just too female. The students' general reaction to the literature was to quickly distance themselves from feminist politics and to declare a non-feminist identity. As Thea said, "I'm not a feminist or even remotely close." Janet stated, "I agree with women getting equal pay, rights, but not just for that, but also for equalness among races, that everyone is equal." Feminism and indeed gender as a category of analysis became something to refuse or resist over the course of the study. The students either failed to reference gender even when it would seem appropriate to do so or simply dismissed it. Zandra stated how irrelevant feminism was to her, "I find a lot of these girls talking about feminist stuff. It's weird. I don't know about the other people, but I don't write about that. I don't think about it."

One of the most dramatic examples of failing to reference gender came from Rebecca who, in replying to a question about what she had learned from the study, commented, "I like to know what other people in Canada are writing, and I like the idea of just experimenting with the form and knowing that there are other forms you can use. I learned things like that." Although the study is explicitly about women writers in Canada, she refused to name the work as that written by women and instead uses the nongendered term "people." In an instance when she was speaking about an experience she had in her film arts class, Rebecca explained, "almost my whole class is boys. There is a couple of girls but they skip a lot." Then she continued, "so I was trying to run this film but people won't show up and things like that and they were really acting immaturely, like, they fool around and we never got the film finished." Despite initially admitting gender as important in understanding her experience, the only time she would do so during the study, Rebecca quickly switched to using words like "people" and "they" rather than continue to highlight gender. It seemed as though she recognized a mistake in naming gender as significant.

The students referred to other forms of oppression rather than address gender oppression. This was most evident when I mentioned that I had overheard a young woman in the school corridors suggest that there is little gender oppression in the world now. Zandra began by commenting on the young woman who expressed the opinion:

Zandra: This person is living in a bubble.
Helen: But you tell me that you don't think about gender oppression that you don't feel oppressed in your own lives. Is that right?
Zandra: Yes, but it still happens in other people's lives. You see it but— [she pauses]
Janet: We just happen to be lucky. (my emphasis)
Zandra: Yeah.
Janet: But I think we realize that people struggle. This school for instance, a fair number of these people can't afford to go to university, can't afford a decent meal. We see this.

Throughout the study issues of class (people can't afford a decent meal), race: (All races are equal), and even age (it's an age thing) were used to suppress specific issues of gender. Often gender oppression was quickly rendered unmentionable, invisible, and insignificant. To use Shoshana Felman's (1982) words, there seemed to be "an active refusal of information" about gender. This refusal to acknowledge gender enabled these young women to see themselves as fortunate, "as lucky." The girls' desire to see themselves as transcending gender and gender oppression, as untouched by a patriarchal world, was powerful. I too found myself experiencing it:

I remember now being caught up in wondering about the "truth" of their statements and the question of false consciousness and my role, which to them must have seemed like Iago whispering some nightmarish story in their ears, and me, too, getting caught somehow, wanting, despite all I know, to believe their words—We're just lucky—to ignore what I know. Clearly my desire to imagine their escape and so perhaps my own from a patriarchal world is at work here suppressing momentarily at least other knowledges.

(My Research Journal)

There are a number of things that seem to anchor the students' reaction to feminism and perhaps my own cited above. It is important to acknowledge the "backlash to feminism" that has occurred in the popular media (Faludi, 1992). This backlash may well be affecting students' responses. As well, the students' views may be reflecting the liberal humanistic discourse that underlies much of school practice and philosophy—a discourse in which fairness and equity mean equal representation, and a balance of perspectives in any exercise is paramount. Clearly the design of the study, with its explicit focus on female students, writers, and experience, ran counter to this. From a liberal perspective, the study was "too female," and there would be a strong need to prevent the discussion from becoming any more female and certainly not more "feminist." As a result students would dismiss gender, and draw attention to other forms of oppression in order to create a balance—in order to be fair. It may be that the students' responses to the feminist work was simply a reflection of an investment in the liberal discourse that may well have dominated their schooling experience.

However, as I suggested in the previous chapters, there was something more fuelling the liberal and antifeminist discourses for these young women. I suspect what intensified their urge toward a so-called balanced perspective was an investment in heterosexuality. Students were not concerned about ignoring, dismissing, or marginalizing men in general. Instead, what ran through the data was a concern for heterosexual relationships—for boyfriends. And this seemed to initiate a kind of rescue mission for men 'who might be lovers'. For example, dispersed throughout the study were comments like Thea's, "I don't find anything wrong with the guys I know," or Janet's: "[The project] might have been about men and how nice they are or even about love or breaking up with a boyfriend." Lauren, who used her journal at various times to write about the kind of men she liked: "I just admire men escially [sic] tall dark masculine men with sexy voices. All of the above are tall, dark, mascule [sic] and have sexy voices, except for Peter. He has beautiful long red hair and hazel eyes." Men were romanticized or idealized in Lauren's comments, perhaps in order to recover them for her in a way that the feminist literature did not. This was clearly at work for Thea as well when she commented again, "I am not a feminist. There is nothing wrong with the guys I know."

The young women in this study seemed to define themselves as women premised on a notion of heterosexuality or what Warner (1993) and Britzman (1995), referred to as "heteronormativity."

Lauren was clearly explaining this to me in her journal when after describing various men in her life or men she would like in her life, she wrote: "Don't worry Helen, I'm not sexually obsessed. I'm just a teenage girl." Lauren forwarded the notion that to be a 'teenage girl' is to be obsessed with men: quite a normal obsession. In a poem in which Janet wrote about her female friends, she too may have been suggesting a similar idea. A section of her poem reads:

> selena talks listens cares shares
> double dates shopping trips shared sports,
> shared men shared dinner

I am not sure what Janet meant by "shared men," but certainly it is a much more powerful position with regard to female heterosexual desire than is usual, in that one is "sharing men" rather than "being shared" by men. It may be that Janet was indicating that she and her friend like the same kind of men, but are not competitive or possessive about them. They 'share' them. Taken more metaphorically, the phrase suggests that part of what might bind Janet and Selena together is that they share "an interest" in men. They share "men." This last possibility suggests that what Janet, Lauren, and the others may have been using primarily to define women as women was an interest in or, more accurately, a desire for men. It was evidently a very important definition that the feminist avant-garde writing seem to have disturbed.

The subject position of "woman" offered in feminist avant-garde literature is not often constructed by heterosexual desire. Apparently for young women claiming a heterosexual identity, such desire precludes other desires from operating in their reading and writing practices. If working with the literature required some degree of identification or recognition of the woman subject, the students needed to relax the prescription of woman or "teenage girl" as constructed through a desire for boys. Relaxing this regulation opens up possibilities of other desires being narrated into existence (e.g., women loving women), unsettling an identity constituted largely and perhaps precariously by heterosexual desire.[3]

The strong efforts of the young women in this study to reinsert heterosexuality into the discussion and into their writing speaks to the incredible power and pleasure of this desire. This study consisted of only twelve sessions, which, in light of the students' entire school program and their lives outside of school, represented only a small amount of time and energy, and yet the students made intense, almost urgent, efforts to work heterosexual desire back into the study. The tension in engaging, even briefly, in literature that excluded explicit heterosexual desire speaks to its power and, perhaps, as well, to its fragility, its vulnerability. The energies marshalled together to ensure that heterosexual desire stayed in the discussion suggests that there may be a serious threat from other, evidently powerful and potentially disruptive, knowledges or desires. What knowledges, desires, and identifications threaten female heterosexual identity.

The literature did provide a place to speak of a same-sex Eros; specifically of pleasure in female relationships. Even though they found the study and the literature "too female," the students did take up the opportunity to write and talk about their female friends and relatives—sisters and mothers—with enthusiasm, and perhaps with some relief. They did write about the problematic nature of some of these relationships, but, by and large, the students wrote poems that celebrated their female friends and maternal relationships. Since these relationships were platonic, this writing did not threaten their investment in heterosexuality. The topic seemed to offer the students a way to make women central in their written work and in their discussions and thus they were able to participate within the premises of feminist avant-garde literature.

Although the young women did expend a great deal of energy inserting heterosexuality into the study, there were a few occasions when they admitted that men were not necessarily worth the effort. Rebecca's frank comment, "I believe that almost all men are scum," Lauren's statement, "Boys are too stupid to do the dishes," and in her journal, "I was really upset. I don't know why, probably over a guy, as usual," suggests that defining oneself outside of heterosexuality was certainly possible, even enticing. The feminist avant-garde poetry may have provided an avenue for this expression. However, it may also have fuelled their desire further. For young women who constitute men as objects of desire and as central in their identity as women, ignoring, dismissing, or admitting that men are problems may feed the desire for the ideal man that inhabits their dreams and fantasies; men that exist in the various texts they're exposed to, like Rebecca's historical fiction and her "Robin Hood" figure or Lauren's "Jackie Collins" romance fictions and her "tall, dark, masculine men with sexy voices." The feminist avant-garde literature may have served to heighten the difference between real (and dismissible) men and ideal symbolic men and thus the desire for the ideal man. Ironically then, the feminist literature may have intensified students' investment in heterosexual desire and its search for the ideal man. And such a search would lead not to feminist literature but to a falling back to literary formations offering idealized heterosexuality with a fantasy man.

Another difficulty with feminism for the young women in my study concerned agency. One of their strongest desires was to see and produce themselves as unaffected by gender, race, or class oppression. As mentioned in the previous chapters, Zandra and Janet spoke of being "lucky" in this regard. With the notable exception of Lauren, students had little sympathy for women characters whom they saw as trapped in oppression, preferring depictions of women as free, and independent in their lives. In this regard the students were very much like the twelve-year-old girls who participated in a study by Meredith Rogers Cherland (1994). The twelve-year-old's deep desire for agency was visible in their reading choices and the texts they recommended to each other as good books.

The desire to be a "dangerous woman" that Zandra articulated would seem to be an implicit wish to have agency in the world. To be dangerous meant for Zandra, acting with stereotypical "male" aggressiveness, intellectually and physically, in opposition to the norm of feminine passivity. For Janet, the rebel persona seemed to offer a potent subject position particularly with regard to sexuality. Lauren described both her own sister and a black female character in Lillian Allen's poem in terms of having agency, as being "powerful" and then commented: "I wish I could be like that."

Feminist avant-garde writing celebrates the subversive efforts of women who actively and assertively write against the literary norms. It would seem to be in line with the students' desires for agency. However, the route to agency in feminist discourses was quite different and difficult for the students to negotiate because it meant first accepting that gender oppression existed for them personally. To admit oneself as subject to oppression may itself produce a loss of agency, and clearly this is not what the young women in the study wished to know or acknowledge. Such knowledge must be actively ignored or renamed as another kind of problem.

Meredith Cherland and Carol Edelsky's research found that specific cultural controls were placed upon girls' desires for agency in the horror fiction that they read. Data suggested that "horror and violence in fiction offered disturbing fantasy experiences that muted and countered the desire for agency. Horror and violence were made attractive when the culture associates them with sexuality, the desire for agency was made to feel dangerous, and the cause of cultural reproduction was served" (1993, p. 36). Considering the daily news, I would not dismiss the possibility that fears concerning violence, perhaps sexual violence, to some degree affected the desire for agency among the young women in my study, but what was more evident was that heterosexuality would seem to be a key factor curbing agency. The version of heterosexuality that seemed to restrict agency associated female passivity and pleasure with heterosexual desire.[4]

Thea's statement, however seriously she meant it, was the most dramatic expression of this version of heterosexual relationships. As cited in a previous chapter, she stated, "I am not a feminist. I don't find anything wrong with the guys I know. I am very indifferent and passive. I don't care about equal rights or wages. I would be completely happy to grow up and get married and be a housewife. I would love that. I am just indifferent to it all." Thea carefully connected passivity (I am very indifferent and passive) to pleasure (I would be completely happy) to heterosexuality (being married and a housewife), which together was linked to a nonfeminist position (I am not a feminist).

This connection played itself out in the students' reading and writing. Denise became irritated when a feminist analysis of a love poem she had brought in to class disrupted her pleasure. The poem written from a male perspective depicted the female character as completing the man; more specifically, as a mirror reflecting back his love. Pleasure, heterosexual romantic love, and passivity (woman as love object) were disrupted by an analysis that pointed out the woman's passivity, with predictable results: the comment from Denise that we should just do a "little bit of analyzing but not like every little thing. . . . It drives me crazy." Rebecca, who declared that she was not a feminist but believed that "almost all men are scum," populated her writing and reading, at least initially, with romantic male characters. For example, she wrote and rewrote versions of Robin Hood in which the female character is abducted then rescued by the male hero, creating or recreating female passivity within heterosexual desire.

The reluctance of the young women to incorporate the kind of innovations, metaphors, story lines they were exposed to suggests a stronger investment in the kind of writing and subject positions offered traditionally. It is not merely that they have been rewarded for displaying competency in these forms, but that their pleasures and desires—their identifications—have been produced within more conventional literary forms. The students refused the options opened up in feminism to be powerful in the world by refuting the efforts of the literature to break the nexus between passivity, pleasure, and femininity.

As indicated in Chapter One, feminist literature seeks to produce alternative representations of femininity outside the boundaries of patriarchal discourses, breaking this connection. This occurs not merely in terms of content and style but also in how writing itself is understood. For the young women in this study, schooled in more conventional notions of creative writing, writing was viewed as distinctly personal, as a place to escape to, as something private to be shared only among the closest of friends or a trusted teacher—what can be thought of as very conventional "feminine" writing. As stated by Rebecca, writing was something done in the private sphere as a hobby—an important hobby, but only a hobby. Women, particularly white middle-class women, have a history of such private writing, and this history and the ideology that supports it was reproduced in the writing curriculum of Britain and its empire in the late nineteenth and early twentieth centuries. It is also an image that is strongly supported by the psychological therapeutic conceptualization of creative writing that focuses on the individual psyche. Furthermore, the best writing, done at home, written literally "laying on her bed," as Denise would tell me, occurred when, according to the young women, emotions were so overpowering that there was a loss of "self" consciousness. This is particularly evident in Rebecca's comment, "I just wrote it without thinking. The pen went by itself almost."

There seems to be passive pleasure and a kind of erotic quality to this understanding and experience of the writing process—the pen moves by itself so Rebecca herself does not need to act. This effortlessness would seem to reproduce the connection between femininity, pleasure, and passivity. This notion of writing is clearly at odds with that promoted in the feminist avant-garde writing, where the process demands an intense and deliberate self-consciousness about gender, language, and literary practices. Furthermore feminist writers anticipate pleasures in writing publicly and subversively, with a passion that lies in the subversion of dominant conventions and images of women—in writing to, for, and about women.

For the young women in my study investments in heterosexuality, which organized desire/pleasure in terms of passivity and femininity; and agency, organized by the denial of oppression, made it difficult to work within the parameters of feminist avant-garde writing. By and large, they refused identification with the "woman" constituted by this literature. Students, at times, used alternative discourses in order to understand and sanction their apparent deployment of feminist avant-garde writing practices. Other times, they simply ignored or dismissed the premises and pleasures offered by feminist avant-garde writing, insisting on more familiar reading and writing practices and pleasures. These more familiar practices and pleasures were constituted within various psychological-therapeutic and/or humanistic discourses on creative writing in which they had been schooled. Even when students did comply with the practices and pleasures of avant-garde writing, it was difficult to get them to acknowledge or discuss it.

However, having said this, I wish to reiterate that the refusal was not easy. The degree of disruption the literature seemed to cause for the students speaks to the difficult contradiction between their desires for heterosexuality requiring "feminine" passivity and for personal agency understood as active "masculine" assertiveness. The active, subversive, male-like "woman" constructed by the feminist literature was enticing because of her agency, no doubt intensifying the contradiction that the young women may have been experiencing. Students' encounter with the feminist avant-garde literature was thus very disturbing. The tension created a demand that the contradiction be denied, forgotten, suppressed, or in some way dealt with. In this case students generally denied the contradiction through an insistence on unproblematic heterosexuality and individual agency.

The Danger of the Avant-Garde:
Unsettling "Good" and "Bad Girl Students"

I have described the "woman" produced in feminist avant-garde writing in a number of contemporary feminist journals of the late 1990s. The "woman" constituted in feminist avant-garde writing is defined in terms of her oppression within gendered (and other) relations of power.[5] Embodied, she is a woman who sees writing and reading as important political acts, who takes pleasure in writing subversively and publicly for women about women. She is actively working against dominant relations of power by subverting language and literary convention to find alternative identities for herself outside of being "man's other." This requires intense self-consciousness about language practices, gender, and other forms of social difference. The lived identities of the students as "writers," "good students," "good girls," and "rebels," allowed them to briefly entertain this "woman" in feminist avant-garde, but ultimately, she placed these identities at risk.

The identities of "good girls," "good students," "writers," "bad girls," or "rebels" are compilations of specific practices, premises, pleasures that are produced and reproduced, with some variation, across a number of discursive fields. Valerie Walkerdine (1989), Carol Gilligan (1990), Michelle Fine and Pat Macpherson (1992), and Nancy Lesko (1988), among others, have described the qualities that constitute these images: conformity, compliancy, and ardent control of the body, voice, emotions, and physicality. In this study the "good girl" identity was in operation, compelling students to remain in the study and attempt to work within the parameters of the feminist avant-garde literature, even when they were not necessarily willing or happy about doing so. Denise explicitly evoked this image or identity when she described why she finally submitted some writing: "I thought I've GOT to do something for her [Helen] or she'll think I'm totally ignoring her." Rebecca, too, expressed this concern: "I think I should let you know I'm not a feminist." It would seem that in order to be fair to me, Rebecca believed she should and does let me know her politics. It would seem the right and polite thing to do, rather than to ignore or mislead someone.

In a different vein, Thea explicitly described herself as a "good student" and then, fearing she sounded conceited, felt she must explain her comment. She later wrote, "I meant good, not only in English but in all my classes, in the sense that I do my homework every night and pull off good enough marks, like, I don't have a problem with whatever my teachers assign. I didn't mean good in the sense that I get awesome marks." For Thea and the others to be a "good student" or more specifically a "good girl" referred to someone who in following the rules, is conscientious, modest, inoffensive. This kind of compliance, while perhaps ensuring their participation in the study, was at odds with the desirable qualities in the "woman" in the feminist writing.

The identity of "writer" displayed most prominently by Rebecca allowed her, and at times the others, to engage with the feminist literature. For Rebecca, the writer was defined, in part, by the desire to know about other writers and writing in general. Rebecca, therefore, wanted to know about "what other people in Canada are writing," to know "that there are other forms you can use." However much as Rebecca might want to "know," writing for her and for the others was formulated largely within traditional discourses, and their investment in these discourses ensured that the "woman" writer in feminist literature was not available or recognizable as a legitimate alternative because a "good" writer and "good" writing are not politicized:

> It was just, like, it didn't really seem like a poem. It was like she just picked a bunch of pictures and then typed the words out. . . It did seem like she kind of threw it together. It almost seems as though she had taken someone else's work and [had] just written something over it. She's, like, manipulating their words. . . It seems like for Women's Liberation or something. It's something you might see—the wall and the graffiti and all that. Well, I guess some poems—poems don't seem like they should be political, I don't know why.

For the students the encounter with feminist writing may have reminded them that "literature" needs to be serious, reverent, and respectful of language and literary conventions, and in particular to transcend its situation and political interests. To be the good girl writer/reader generally meant not highlighting gender oppression or marking oneself as gendered. Hilary Davis (1993) described "the good and bad girl" reader in reader-response theory:

> Mainstream reader-response theory dichotomizes the women reader as either "disembodied" or "embodied," either a good girl or a bad girl reader. Women readers are viewed as angels, monsters, or amazons. Yet these images require that patriarchy acknowledge the reader as a woman thus violating its own definitions for "woman" and "readers." Within androcentric reader-response theory the majority of women readers are invisible. Women readers masquerade as disembodied in an attempt to "pass" as legitimate readers. (p. 45)

To be seen as a legitimate writer/reader, Rebecca and the others needed to avoid becoming embodied. It was difficult therefore to take up the subject position in feminist avant-garde writing that demands or highlights the presence of the woman; more specifically, a woman's body. Also since in feminist avant-garde it is a body which does not link heterosexual desire, passivity, and pleasure, it also means highlighting a "wrong" or "transgressing" female body. So while the identity or subject position of the writer allowed Rebecca to work with the literature, at the same time it assured her refusal of the "woman" writer constituted in feminist avant-garde literature.

Unlike the others, the desire to be a "dangerous women," to be a "bad girl," did not seem problematic for Janet. As I described previously, she seemed to take great pleasure in defining herself as a rebel as evident when I asked her about which poems she liked:

Helen: Which [poem from the project] do you really like now?
Janet: I like the ones that have swearing in them. [She laughs]
Helen: Why?
Janet: 'Cause it's something that school doesn't allow.

This desire and pleasure in breaking rules allowed Janet to more exuberantly work with the literature and its construct of "woman." Although Janet broke with language and literary standards, in terms of themes, particular in terms of feminist or gendered themes, the feminist literature did not seem to offer her a particularly enticing place from which to write. While Janet could produce the bad girl or the rebel by breaking language convention and criticizing teachers and schooling, the issues of gender remained unpalatable or unnecessary for her to take on. Indeed Janet, while endorsing the literature to some degree, seemed to resist the kind of rule-breaking opportunities it offered.

In this instance the desire to be a "good writer," "good girl," "good student," or "rebel," in addition to their pleasure in female friendships and maternal relations, may have allowed the young women to negotiate with the premises, practices, and pleasures of feminist avant-garde writing. In fact this particular confluence may have compelled students to dance, albeit briefly, with the "woman" constituted in feminist writing. But ultimately the construction of femininity, heterosexual desire, and agency organized within the identities of "good girl readers and writers" and "female rebels" made their encounter with the literature dangerous and unsettling. These constructions form boundary markers, or forcelines, that students negotiated with and against during their experience of feminist avant-garde writing.[6] While such markers might be reconstituted in any feminist pedagogical intervention, when limned against the backdrop of humanistic and therapeutic discourses concerning creative writing they were all the more visible, and for the young women in my study, all the more contentious.

Female Adolescent Identification and Desire

I suggested in the introduction to this text that one of the major challenges of adolescents is to distance oneself from parents and siblings and affirm a sexual identity (and love object) outside the family. Adolescent girls face the additional challenge of reorganizing a more complex relationship to language and, more generally, to Western culture where "female" or "femininity" is viewed as aberrant. I posited that intense identification may be a predictable adolescent response to the loss of the early parent-child relationship as they distance themselves from the family. Identification may also be at work in the specific struggles of young women with Western culture. It may account, in part at least, for the power of the investment of the young women in this study in feminine or disembodied writing and their repudiation, albeit conflicted, of feminist writing practices.

According to psychoanalytic theory, our first most profound identifications involve parents. This history may be organized such that the "father" represents public culture, civilization, and the status quo, for it is he who, in the traditional organization of the family, travels from the family to the public sphere and back again. He provides a route out of the family. The father is the "knight in shining armor" because he comes from "outer space" and brings the excitement of outsidedness, uncontaminated by conflicts around maternal dependency (Benjamin, 1995, p. 122).

Seeking separation from the parents of childhood, adolescents might well attempt to retrace his route, following his path, learning his knowledge, attempting to find themselves within a masculine tradition. This history may be organized in actual family relations, certainly in those families that follow traditional middle-class gendered roles and relations. But even in families where the mother may work outside the home, this involvement in the public sphere may be seen as incidental to her domestic role. She may be viewed as a mere interloper in the public sphere and therefore unacceptable as a guide for adolescents desperately seeking a world outside of the family.

But even if the parents participate both in public and private spheres in ways that are validated, the gendered pattern of private and public domains are apparent in many social and cultural narratives. Often the father is symbolically or literally encoded as the representative of the public sphere, as an independent, exciting, insider/outsider to the family. Stories and images of a public mother are far less frequent. Feminism, and more specifically feminist writing also appears to offer separation from the family, but it is routed through a phallic "mother" who writes publicly and subversively. Either options require strong acknowledgement of and identification with either the public father or mother.

If identification with the father organizes a route away from the family then a young woman's independence and her search for someone outside of the family is placed at some risk if this identification is thwarted. However, even in these times, strong identification with the father is not often encouraged in the daughter. In the case of the mother, strong identification is encouraged, but it is often the domestic mother with whom one is expected to identify. Identification with the public mother—for example, the feminist mother—provides a route away from the family of childhood, but also away from traditional Western culture where the mother would have no public voice, where speaking would only be seen as aberrant or eccentric. It is an extraordinarily difficult situation for young women. In light of such difficulty, it is not surprising that the strategies of feminine writing or disembodied writing appeared to offer the young women in this study a far less risky means of reconciling femininity and Western culture(s).

Identification may well be a factor in the organization of female heterosexuality and the search for an "other" from outside the family. Sexual identity, according to Freud, is organized in relation to the nature of attachment with parents. The attainment of heterosexuality is dependent on the child identifying with the same-sex parent and desiring the other as love object (1964b). For Freud, female heterosexuality means identifying with her mother and transferring her desire from her mother to her father. In this I believe Freud falsely assumed a strict separation between desire and identification and a rigid polarity between what mothers and fathers offer their children.[7] He also assumed bisexuality as an originary preoedipal state and therefore homosexuality as an immature identity and heterosexuality as a later and more developed sexual identity.[8] Instead, as Diana Fuss (1995), and Jessica Benjamin (1995, 1988), among others, have pointed out, identification and desire may be operating with relationship to both parents and that sexual orientation may have a less essentialized nature.

For the young woman claiming a heterosexual identity, the task, it would seem, is to assure a focus on the father as a primary object of desire and secondly to secure the substitution of the father with a male (real or symbolic) from outside the family. This task is done in a context of swaying tensions between maternal and paternal desire and identification. If desire and identification are not entirely separate, and if identifications and identities (including sexual identity) are fluid, partial, social, contradictory and nonunified, then this task is immensely complex and incomplete.

One route through the quagmire of desire and identification for young women might be to first ensure the mother's unavailability as a love object by insisting on her heterosexuality. If the mother is named as heterosexual, then the daughter's desire for the mother is thwarted. This desire is redirected to the father. In this way the "good mother" might be seen as one who insists on her own heterosexuality thus pushing the daughter, despite herself, to the father and to heterosexuality. The feminist literature did not act as the "good mother." Instead the writing reminds readers of the pleasure of identification with and desire for women and perhaps for the first woman we knew—our mother. This might in part explain the hostility of the students towards the feminist literature and their intense efforts, in the absence of their "mother's" affirmation of heterosexuality, to affirm so stridently their own heterosexuality.

The daughter's second move must be to deflect her focus on her father as love object in accordance with the incest taboo. She must find her sexual object-choice from outside the family. Possibly this might be achieved by intensifying her identification with the father which would then diminish his status as a love object and force the search elsewhere. If agency is one quality that safely distinguishes the father from the mother in a patriarchal society, it could serve as an important and very attractive basis of identification with the father. The "good father" will insist on his agency and on his daughter's, just as the daughter will stress both his and her own agency. Since the patriarchal power and agency of the father is challenged in feminism(s) it is not surprising that young women claiming hetero-sexual identity found the literature unsettling. The more maternal identification, desire, and agency are promoted, the more impossible it is to claim agency as the grounds for paternal identification. The more gender polarity is challenged the more precariously gender and sexual identity may appear and the more disturbing the experience with the feminist avant-garde may be.

There are complications with identification with the father. If the daughter identifies strongly with the father she runs the "risk" of incorporating his desires—including presumably his heterosexual desires for the mother. As Diana Fuss comments, "What is identi-fication if not a way to assume the desires of the other?" (1995, p. 12). This threatens the daughter's heterosexual desire, revealing its fragility, and rendering her ambivalent about identification with the father and his agency.

The young women in this study reiterated their agency through-out the study, but they were not unequivocal. They may have seen themselves as like their fathers, but they also spoke of being "lucky" compared to other people; presumably other women. The word "lucky woman" is an amazing designation. It allowed the young women to identify with their fathers or men in terms of agency, and to disconnect themselves from unlucky, oppressed women, like their mothers or at least women. At the same time the term "lucky wo-men" retains a notion of women as passive and without agency to which the students are only tenuously linked as lucky "women." "Lucky women" functioned as a new category—a third gender, if you will. Furthermore, the identity or category "lucky woman" oc-curred by chance rather than design so the young women need not claim the identity or politics of the feminist. Thus, the feminist "woman" produced in avant-garde literature—"the unlucky, oppressed woman"—can be safely ignored as irrelevant.

The same as her father in terms of power and agency, the same as her mother in terms of heterosexuality, the heterosexual adolescent daughters shift her desire to one who is different, that is, to a male (symbolic or actual) from outside the family. This love object is socially outside the family, but in every sense created by the family. And this route or pattern, materially and discursively constructed, while not unproblematic itself, may be sufficiently helpful in securing sexuality that the young women insist upon it. However, this route of desire and identification is precarious enough to be disturbed by even a brief encounter with feminist avant-garde literature, even for young women who, nearing the end of adolescence, have struggled for some time with the challenges of female adolescence.

Clearly the pleasure and fun of flirting with boys, of "sharing" men, the pleasure and power in thinking that the world is yours, that you are indeed a "lucky" heterosexual woman, seemed to be placed at considerable risk in this encounter with the wild words of feminist avant-garde texts. The costs of identification with the woman in feminist writing may simply be too high, too dangerous, to an identity that already seems too precariously constructed.

I do not wish to suggest that this is the only explanation for the responses of the young women in this study; nor do I wish to suggest that this is the only pattern or route of identification and desire available for heterosexual female adolescents generally or for those in this study specifically. Instead I offer this interpretation as one place to begin to understand the complex psychic and social environment which feminist pedagogical interventions may often expose, disturb, and produce.

The "Lucky (Heterosexual) Woman": The Threat to a Feminist Haven

The young women in my study brought a history of identifications and desires to their encounter the feminist avant-garde literature. They also had to contend with my history and previous identifications. My history, as I have come to think of it, must include my identification with the literature and the "woman" it constitutes, as well as my pedagogical desires to create a feminist haven in patriarchal academia, in effect offering a kind of "rescue" of female students. Certainly, the study was designed to create a women's space in the English curriculum: a space to transgress traditional school reading and writing practices by exploring alternative texts and reading/writing strategies, with a specific focus on the inscription of gender difference. In creating this space, I drew on the history of feminist literary criticism and women's studies, organizing what I saw as a "feminist enclave at the edge of the patriarchal academic empire" without male students or male colleagues (Easton, 1989).

The separatist politics that underlie this version of feminism and feminist criticism are based on the development of female solidarity. The students' insistence on reinscribing traditional notions of heterosexual desire and of individual agency disrupted, to varying degrees, the possibility of creating a feminist "haven." Invoking heterosexual desire supported a female identity predicated on male sexual attention and a view of other women as competitors for such attention. This threatened group solidarity and a feminist politics which seeks alternative definitions of woman. An insistence on personal agency defeated the need for the power of group affiliation. The notion of literature as gender neutral, as capable of transcending issues of power and politics, disrupted the need for and the importance of feminist literary scholarship. In light of this, it was perhaps not surprising that my work and identity as a feminist teacher was challenged in this experience.

As the study progressed I found myself questioning my role as a rescuer. This study was indeed built upon the premise that female students need a curricular rescue organized through alternative textual practices in the hope that young women might more easily connect or identify with such alternatives. My own personal history of schooling, my previous identifications with and against teachers, feminist and otherwise, no doubt contributed to this desire. It is important as well to acknowledge the social side to this seemingly personal fantasy. Educational discourse, both popular and official, is replete with rescue fantasies. These discourses are heavily populated by actual or symbolic teacher-heroes who, through their own in-dividual efforts, "save" students from an evil society, or from incompetent, uncaring parents or from cruel or inept teachers, and/or from a corrupt educational system that threatens the minds and souls of students (Robertson, 1997a, 1997b). Historically, English teachers in particular have been portrayed as "Preachers of Culture" with a special calling to build the character of students through the study of literature, and, in the interests of social justice, develop students' literary and linguistic competency, thereby increasing their social mobility (Mathieson, 1975). The image of the teacher as rescuer or savior appears not only in educational documents, but in popular culture. Judith Robertson (1997a) has delineated three archetypal teacher-heroes that appear in popular films: the "Lone Ranger," the "Angel of the School House," and "Cassandra." Robertson found in these archetypes, and in female student teachers' responses to popular teacher films, desires for and fantasies of love and devotion between teacher and students.

I do wonder about the teacher's need for affirmation—that students love their teacher-rescuer. It is important to acknowledge the limits of such fantasies for feminist education and how the relationship of rescuer to the rescued hierarchically organizes power. This does not diminish the importance of meeting the needs of students, but acknowledging this fantasy can help explain the shock, anger, and/or disappointment, when students refuse to play out the fantasy—who refuse rescue.

Although I have in this research repeatedly focused on the identificatory possibilities of "the woman" produced in feminist avant-garde writing, there was another "woman" present in the class. Although I did not name myself explicitly as a feminist educator, undoubtedly students inferred as much, perhaps at times seeing in me the embodiment of the woman produced in the literature. I do know that at the very least I have always preferred, perhaps actively sought, my students' affirmation, if not affection. The challenges I posed to students directly or indirectly in the pedagogy and literature offered in this study meant that such affirmation was not always possible. Indeed at times I believe I was viewed as the representation of feminism and the critique was personal and difficult, as evident in Denise's frustrated comment, "Every time I see you, it's like, I'm not that creative. **You've** killed my creative juices. I can't think any more."

Considering that adolescents seek to distance themselves from their former love objects—their parents—yet at the same time remain in a dependent relationship with them, and considering that any love object will invoke but ultimately fail to satisfy desire, it follows that child-parent relations will be complex, volatile, and fraught with contradiction (A. Freud, 1971). It is not surprising that adolescents love and hate, accept and reject their parents, or that they will love and hate, accept, and reject their parental substitutes. And obviously teachers can be positioned easily as substitutes for parents invoking similar autonomy/dependency issues. This also has a social or cultural component, for adolescents are often portrayed in the media as in perpetual conflict with their parents and at times their teachers. This normalization of a "generation gap" may also have a role to play in how adolescents make sense of their experience with parents and other adults.

It has been argued that the teacher-student relationship, like the relationship between analysand and analyst, can recreate traumatic events through transference (Kelly, 1997; Gallop, 1995). In this study the loss of relations between parent and child, between women and Western public culture, the complex relationship of women to language, and more generally, the relationship between feminism and young women may have been played out at moments in the teacher-student relationship, as the students and I worked our way through the study. The relationship of student to teacher, more specifically, the identificatory possibilities offered by "the feminist teacher" was not the focus of this study, but this relationship is worth further analysis.

The Availability of Alternative Dreams and Desires: Alternative Identities and Identifications

It may well be that for many adolescents the pathways of identification and desire will be in some way threatened in an encounter with feminist avant-garde writing. These pathways, in turn, will threaten the routes of identification and desire that underlie feminist political and pedagogical work. Certainly the responses of the young women to the literature indicates the depth of their affective and intellectual investments in literature and a self that feminist educators should not ignore. It is also apparent that the availability of subject positions may be largely dependent on our identifications and the affective investments they support. Resisting or embracing the "woman" in feminist avant-garde writing or indeed any subject position may be determined at least in part by rational choices, concerns, and interests; however, what will hold and name a position is the affect—desire. Indeed desire or a particular configuration of desires may well name or define the subject position. Thus, a woman may not be named or recognized as a "woman" if she desires another woman, desires independence, etc. These desire(s) may be what makes her appear as a legitimate "woman" to society. Race, class, gender, ethnicity, nationality could also be defined in terms what one desires. Deeply invested in particular desires, it may be very difficult for an individual (or a society) to entertain change.

Identification and desire may be what lies at the heart of institutions, such as schools (Corrigan, 1990). If identifications and desires are to some degree produced or conditioned by reading and writing practices, then within school contexts, language, and literature classrooms lie at the very core of their inscription or reinscription. That is, identification and desire are central to English Studies (language and literature) classrooms. Such a view shifts English Studies from a study of the literary canon and linguistic structure and mechanics to a cultural studies model in which the discursive organization of subjectivity is central (O'Neill, 1992; Morgan, 2000, 1993).[9] This study confirms the importance of placing affective investments on the agenda of language and literature curricula and viewing these investments as central in any emancipatory educational project. This means examining both the desires, dreams, and pleasures in which we are invested and what those investments suppress or permit, in the hope of gaining some measure of control over the direction of our desiring. Peter McLaren writes:

> Yet it is necessary to acknowledge that the capacity of individuals to at least partially recognize the constitution of the self, is what makes liberation possible. . . . It is also a precondition for refleshment, or forming a space of desire where we can assume self-consciously and critically new modes of subjectivity hospitable to a praxis of self and social empowerment. We must never forget that we can act in ways other than we do. (1990, p. 163)

This means providing a space for students and teachers to explore the contradictions and implications of their desiring. As Deborah Britzman notes:

> Students bring to the classroom contradictory desires. Unless they have opportunities to explore these desires as contradictory and in relation to culture, social structure, history and one another, and in relation to their own proximity to the histories and experiences of racism and sexism, they are apt to continue to dismiss education along with its irrelevant models. (1993, p. 39)

In this study the young women were presented with an alternative literary formation that provided an alternative education in desire, pleasure and identification. Although the feminist literature did seem to map onto the desire and pleasure of female friendships and maternal relationships, the literature evidently did not map onto students' investments in personal agency and most importantly onto heterosexual desire, particularly where femininity was linked with passivity and pleasure. The literature, despite its transgressive characteristics, did not generally offer a place for students to take up their current version of heterosexual desire, explore its contradictions, and potentially rework it. If a wide range of identities is to be made available to young women, then exploring and reworking current desires and dreams will need to be done.

Yet at the same time I wonder at the statement made by Bronwyn Davies:

> If I were the kind of unitary rational being that liberal humanists once convinced most of us we were, then to the extent that my "feminist" desire contradicts "feminine" desire, the feminist would undo the feminine. But our patterns of desire are organized in terms of our gendered identity such that rational attention to the contradiction is not sufficient to undo it. (1990, p. 501)

Like Davies, I am not confident about rational efforts to change desire, but it would seem that until we find some better means all we can do is interrogate the desires, dreams, or pleasures in which we are invested. It seems unlikely that one can simply unlearn desires and pleasures by replacing them with alternative (and better?) desires and pleasures. At least, this study suggests not. But while it may not be possible to simply unlearn desires and pleasures merely through substitution, it may be possible to defuse them in some sense by increasing the kinds of desires and pleasures (and subject positions) open to women by exploring the contradictions in our current investments and their discursive and material production in our lives. After that, it may be a case of working creatively with identification and desire: feminine, feminist, or otherwise, in order to entertain or indeed imagine other identities, other possibilities, than those currently authorized within school contexts and society, to offer what Roger Simon (1992) calls " A Pedagogy of Possibility." This will be no mean feat for teachers and educators committed to transformative education, equity and social justice in the political climate that faces us all in the new millennium.

Disturbing Intervention: Feminist Writing and Teaching

> If new content in whatever form does not map onto the crucial issues of desire, then we should not be surprised if it fails as an intervention.
>
> —Valerie Walkerdine (1987)

I am still convinced of the value of feminist avant-garde writing in English/LA and Creative Writing classrooms committed to socially transformative work. But its value may not lie in its ability to supply an immediate springboard to producing subversive texts and subject positions, as much as it does in its ability to disrupt and make visible our investments in dominant subject positions and conceptions of writing, literature, and social difference. I believe that the disruptive possibilities this literature offers needs to be heightened. To use feminist avant-garde literature more effectively would require a shift in two directions. One direction is towards greater complexity. As surprising as it might sound considering the nature of feminist avant-garde writing, there needed to be more "wildness in the words." The work needs to be noisier. As Jane Flax writes

> Feminist theorists, like other postmodernists, should encourage us to tolerate, invite, and interpret ambivalence, ambiguity, and multiplicity as well as to expose the roots of our needs for imposing order and structure no matter how arbitrary and oppressive these may be.
>
> (1990, p. 183)

If feminist avant-garde writing is indeed open to subversive thinking and to redefinition of "woman," then there is room, at least potentially, for exploring and reinscribing heterosexual desire. This was not evident in the literature being produced at the time of the study. This may be due to a reification of "man as problem" in the literature. Viewing man as oppressor of or problem for woman makes it difficult to rework heterosexual desire since such desire would mean loving the enemy. So that, while "woman" was more open to redefinition, the category of "man" and "heterosexuality" was not.

Besides ensuring that there is more wildness in the literature, the focus in the high school classroom needs to be on the pluralities, complexities, ambiguities, and contradictions that exist in the investments and identity formations of young women's lives. Attention needs to focus back to complex investments evident in the negotiations of students with the literature. It is the negotiations that need to become the pedagogical material, so that the lesson is not on the alternative literary form per se, but on the exploration of investments that become evident as one negotiates with text.

The second direction required in order to use feminist avant-garde writing more effectively is towards greater historicization. The explicit historicization of literary formations, including feminist avant-garde writing, and the subject positions constituted in these formations, might have made the literature more legitimate. Students need the opportunity to investigate not only what alternative literary formations offer, but also what is produced by conventional writing—how our investments are inscribed in conventional or more traditional the reading and writing practices. In this study the emphasis on participating in the literary formation of feminist avant-garde writing meant that progressive and classical models of writing were left largely unnamed and unexplored. Thus, the more familiar traditions in which students were operating could easily be seen as natural and normal, lying outside of history and politics; whereas feminist avant-garde writing could be viewed as something unnatural and abnormal. The power of feminist avant-garde as a site of poetic language "where language is at its most radical in its refusal to take itself for granted" needed to be more explicitly directed back at the progressive and classical discourses of creative writing (Min-Ha, 1992, p. 154).

An aspect that was missing in the selections of feminist writing used in the study but apparent in the young women's own writing was fantasy. Rebecca, Denise, Zandra, and Lauren often used creative writing as a place for fantasy. As noted earlier, Valerie Walkerdine has suggested that fantasy can operate as a vehicle for the relatively safe exploration of difficult conflicts and uncomfortable emotions. The expressive realism of the poems offered in the study did not allow students such explorations. The potential of fantasy to allow for revisioning—for writing wildness—and its potential for allowing greater exploration of desire and suppressed knowledges was untapped. Obviously fantasy may allow an individual to safely sidestep current identities in exploring difficult struggles and problems. Thus it may offer an easier route to negotiate alternative subject positions and one's current affective investments than feminist avant-garde writing. The potential of feminist science fiction and fantasy genre would seem worth investigating. As well, the potential of multi-voice narrated writing also needs to be examined further. Poems with this characteristic were enthusiastically received by the students in this study and several attempted to use multiple narrators in their own writing. Writing that fragments a single authoritarian telling, like multi-voiced narration or multiple storytellers, may allow for a wider acknowledgement of the contradictions, multiplicities, and ambiguities in one's life. This acknowledgement may help to destabilize established subjectivities enough to allow the writer/reader to explore them and perhaps to imagine if not access alternatives. Pedagogically, feminist literature that featured narrative fragmentation and/or fantasy may prove to be a valuable textual resource in opening up the range of possibilities for young women.

What is also apparent in the data is that in almost all cases students produced more conflicted, complex renderings of their positioning in their own creative writing than they did in the interviews, class discussions, or even in their journal writing. Rebecca, for example, explicitly addressed gender in her last poem, despite the fact she could not easily do so in conversation. Thea and Janet wrote about female friendships in their poetry, despite the fact that they repeatedly disavowed the importance of focus on women. Denise played, to some degree, with literary convention in her own writing, despite the fact she repeatedly claimed it was not her "style." It may be simply that they were complying with the demands of the class, but I suspect that in creative writing there exist greater possibilities for play and fantasy, and that that together with the destabilizing aspects of writing generally, freed students to a greater extend than did other forms of expression. It may be that feminist pedagogy might do well to examine further creative writing/composition as a vehicle for transformative education.

Finally, although I have no concrete evidence to support this claim, I suspect that the young women in my study may have wished to inscribe heterosexual desire into the study, not only because this desire was enticing and important in their identification as young women and writers, but, also, because they feared the alternative—homosexual desire. If we configure lesbianism as Adrienne Rich's (1980) "lesbian continuum" in which all women may be configured as "spiritually or metaphorically" lesbians, then the feminist literature for women about women may be construed as a kind of lesbian practice. Since the term "lesbian" is still a derogatory term in school corridors, it would be surprising if the young women in the study were not concerned about this label.

Yet if "lesbianism" operates, as Monique Wittig suggests, as a sign of the possibility of radical change in women's lives, or what Katie King calls "feminism's magical sign," the "sign of something "entirely new" for both lesbians and non-lesbians," then this needs to be acknowledged (1986, p. 83). The power in this sign for straight women rests in how it disrupts the identity of woman. Wittig writes:

> What is a woman? . . . . Frankly it is a problem that lesbians do not have because of a change of perspective, and it would be incorrect to say that lesbians associate, make love, live with women, for "woman" has meaning only in heterosexual systems of thought and heterosexual economic system. (1990, p. 3)

Remembering this "non-woman" may help straight women to disrupt the notion of "woman" within heterosexual economies that constitute them as passive. In the English classroom this might mean including "gay and lesbian" literature on the curriculum.[10] As evident in this study a less controversial possibility is to focus on female friends and maternal relationships since these relationships may be configured to some degree outside of heterosexuality. However, first and foremost, the concerns and fears of young women about homosexuality need to be addressed. There is too much silence in curriculum already about this issue which works to the detriment of students of all sexualities and their teachers.

Obviously much of what I am suggesting here may make for disruptive and unsettling pedagogical experiences. If one accepts Roland Barthes' distinction between texts of bliss, and texts of pleasure, as described in Chapter One, I continue to promote the potential of text of bliss—a text that "imposes a state of loss, the text that discomforts . . . .[that] unsettles the reader's historical, cultural, psychological assumptions" as opposed to a text that "grants euphoria: the text that comes from culture and does not break with it, [that] is lined to a comfortable practice of reading" (1975, p. 17). However, considering the power of identification, effective feminist pedagogy might also mean providing texts of pleasure that would support a feminist emancipatory project. For the young women in my study invested in heterosexual desire and personal agency, this may mean providing texts that offer neither the traditional heterosexual sensibilities as offered in the standard school literature, nor the lesbian sensibilities offered in the feminist avant-garde literature, but instead female bisexuality, perhaps symbolically inscribed as motif, metaphor, image, character, or as story line in text. If such characters and texts exist, I believe that they would have provided a better place for identification. Feminist science fiction literature, for example, may have been appropriate for the group of young women in my study. Works like Joanna Russ' (1975) *The Female-Man,* or Marge Piercy's (1976) *Woman on the Edge of Time,* offer fantasies in which bisexuality is an organizing theme or motif.

Of course what is also required is a pedagogical method that would be suitable for feminist texts and for the interrogation demanded by feminist emancipatory work. The literary texts, and readers' negotiation with such texts were the focus of this study, but certainly pedagogy needs to be addressed in future research. To develop such a pedagogy, and many efforts are underway to do so, will require future theorizing of affective investments, particularly the operation of desire in literary experience. In this study negotiating with the feminist literature, that is, with the "woman" constituted in the writing, was defined, in part, by the expression of similarity or the desire to be the same as a character offered in the writing. This identification seems appropriate for texts of pleasure but not for those of bliss, as these texts are described by Roland Barthes.

The condition of identification or "enfleshment" that Peter McLaren describes is dependent upon an unproblematic correspondence between reader and character. Successful identification requires that the desire to be the "other" be met somehow. In other words, identification requires the pleasure of finding of what is familiar between self and other. This pleasure is not possible with the unsettling texts of bliss which destablize readers' sense of themselves. This text explored the investments of a group of young women that affected identification with feminist avant-garde texts. This was done in an effort to understand and expand the range of identities possible for young women within a feminist emanicpatory agenda. As I see it now, part of such work would lie in finding a pedagogy suitable for alternative reading pleasures/desires, using a notion of identification. Hilary Davis' (1993) notion of reading for "shared anotherness" would seem promising for such efforts. Rather than reading for a narcissistic absorption of the 'other' [a shared anotherness] seeks communication and communion rather than domination and appropriation" (p. 133). The self-reflexivity required of Davis' reading strategy focuses on the recognition of both similarity and difference. In this study Lauren seemed to capture this recognition in a way that supported a feminist politics when she indicated her desire to be like a particular character in one of the feminist poems—"I wish I could be like that." This phrase, which haunts me still, reflects the inadequacy of McLaren's notion of identification. The desire or wish to be "like" a character does not provide for successful identification according to McLaren's definition since the individual acknowledges a difference between herself and the subject position—a lack. Yet Lauren's "improper or unsuccessful" identification seems to be a useful place for transformative feminist pedagogy to begin. Exploring difference and similarity, fuelled by a desire for similarity and/or difference in what one has or wants would seem potent grounds for rereading texts. Clearly a more complex understanding of identification and desire is required in order to use Barthes' texts of bliss and pleasure.

And Finally

I am still astounded at the intensity of the response of the young women to the writing they read and produced, particularly considering the fact that the study consumed relatively little energy or time in the lives of the students. I am amazed at how difficult and destabilizing the experience was, and as a result I continue to be amazed at the power of reading and writing acts to destabilize or disrupt identity and desire. Clearly if we wish to expand possibilities, in particular to make alternative subject positions truly available to young women (and to ourselves), one route lies in reading and writing practices.

Having said all this, I must confess I have a great deal of uncertainty about what is possible in the feminist classroom. Identification seems all too intense a process; and the powerful associations of passivity, pleasure, femininity, and heterosexuality difficult to undercut. These are dangerous associations, complicating as well as constraining urgent desires for personal agency in the world. I worry that the move to greater complexity in teaching: to greater attention to ambiguity and contradiction, to the affect that runs through identity and identifications that I have suggested here, may leave feminist discourses vulnerable to paralyzing ambivalence or to a domestication or reinscription within dominant ideologies. As suggested by Alison Jones (1993):

> The old dichotomies led to clear explanations and impetus for action, the new complexities may have the opposite effect. As Joan Cocks puts it: "Can a militant oppositional effort be sparked by complex, not simple, ideas? Or is the power of simple ideas a necessary stimulus to rebellion? Is disillusionment, then—when life ultimately is found to be complicated, not simple—rebellion's necessary end?" (p. 165)

It is also important to remember to that these are not easy times in which to be a feminist teacher (Coulter, 1995). It is true that the effect of feminist literary theory has been profound in English Studies. The development of feminist literary criticism, the rereading of the canon, the rediscovery of forgotten texts and authors, and the promotion of new texts and authors, have pumped fresh air into the study of literature. And although university campuses remain chilly climates for most women, women's studies programs generally, and feminist literary criticism specifically, have gained a certain degree of respectability in the academy. But ironically, as North American feminist theory has become relatively secure, feminism as a social movement has encountered major setbacks in a climate of new conservatism. Indeed, as Jane Gallop comments, "in the American academy feminism gets more and more respect while in the larger society women cannot call themselves feminists" (1993, p. 63).

It is with good reason then I worry about destabilizing feminist identity even further. Part of this my be my fear in destabilizing my own identity, that is my own investments—to lose myself as the quotations at the outset of this chapter suggest. And yet to stabilize feminism into another orthodoxy is clearly not the answer, no matter how comforting that can be personally and/or politically. Perhaps it is a matter of learning to live with uncertainty, and for me, perhaps for you, certainly for our students, to remember the "dance," "the laughter," "the unholy babble of speech," that is, the pleasure in transgressive reading and writing practices—the joy in "letting wildness" into our words, and into our lives.

Notes

Introduction: Letting Wildness Into the Words (pp. 1–14)

1. I am using the term *avant-garde* rather than experimental or innovative writing simply because the term is used most frequently in literary and academic journals. Also I wish to retain a connection between the writing currently being produced in this genre and the history of women producing avant-garde writing in the early 20th century and before. This rich but largely ignored history will be briefly outlined in Chapter One. For a more extensive discussion see Ellen Friedman & Miriam Fuchs' 1989 text, *Breaking the Sequence: Women's Experimental Fiction,* Princeton: Princeton University Press. For an excellent examination of the feminist avant-garde writing in Quebec, see Karen Gould's 1990 text, *Writing in the Feminine: Feminism and Experimental Writing in Quebec,* Carbondale: Southern Illinois University Press.

2. The terms *identity* and *subject position* are not synonymous. I am using subject position to refer to a specific discursive configuration of the self. Identity is a more global sense of the self that emerges in the adoption of one or more subject positions over time. *Identification* is a psychoanalytic term referring to a process whereby individuals see themselves as co-terminous or identical with a subject position.

3. All the participants in the study have been given pseudonyms. The students chose their own pseudonyms.

Chapter One: Feminist Writing Practices: Wild Women/ Wild Words (pp. 15–32)

1. An excellent review of the research literature on gender and language is offered in Deborah Cameron's introduction to her 1998 edited text, *The Feminist Critique of Language: A Reader,*

Neely Ayim's 1997 text, *The Moral Parameters of Good Talk: A Feminist Analysis*, Waterloo, Ontario: Wilfrid Laurier University Press, 1997, offers an excellent review of language as moral practice. A more focused linguistic analysis of gendered language practices is offered in the chapters of Jennifer Coates' edited 1998 text, *Language and Gender: A Reader*, Oxford: Blackwell.

2. It is important to acknowledge that feminist avant-garde writing as configured within major feminist literary journals in Canada during the 1980s was largely a 'white women's project." Efforts to be more inclusive have been made, but it has not been easy. Some of the early and ongoing tensions are captured in the 1990 text, *Telling It: Women and Language Across Cultures,* edited by The Telling It Book Collective, Vancouver: Press Gang.

Chapter Two: The Scene of Writing and Research (pp. 33–44)

1. There are a number of excellent texts that address feminist research methods and methodologies. Three of these include Sandra Harding's (1987) edited text *Feminism and Methodology*, Bloomington: Indiana University Press; Dorothy Smith's (1987) *The Everyday World as Problematic: A Feminist Sociology*; Boston: Northeastern University Press; and Patty Lather's (1991) text *Getting Smart: Feminist Research and Pedagogy With/in the Postmodern*, London: Routledge.

Chapter Three: Threatening the Good Writer (pp. 45–66)

1. I asked Rebecca if this poem was directed at me. She assured me it was not. I suspect Rebecca did not position me as teacher.

Chapter Four: Threatening the Good Student (pp. 67–88)

1. Betty was a Caucasian student who was a close friend of Thea's. Originally in the study, Betty left when her timetable was changed such that she could no longer attend her creative writing class and use that class time to participate in the project.

Chapter Five: Threatening the Rebel (pp. 89–108)

1. Heteronormativity refers the idea that heterosexuality is often assumed to be a universal experience. As the standard or norm, its practices are expected and valued (Britzman, 1995; Warner, 1993).

Chapter Seven: Dangerous Desires: Disturbing Identifications (pp. 137–168)

1. An earlier version of this chapter appeared in Sharon Todd's (1997) text *Learning Desire: Perspectives on Pedagogy, Culture and the Unsaid,* New York: Routledge, pp. 140–161. See also Helen Harper "Reading, identity and desire: High school girls and feminist avant-garde literature," *Journal of Curriculum Theorizing,* 12 (1996): 6–13, and for a related discussion focused on feminist literary criticism see, Helen Harper, "Dangerous desires: Feminist literary criticism in high school English class," *Theory into Practice,* (1998b), 220–228.

2. These comments were made in response to presentations at two conferences: The Canadian Society for Studies in Education, Kingston, Ontario, Canada and "Research and/in Teaching," St. Patrick's College, Dublin, Ireland.

3. I am not suggesting here that the students' sexual orientation was in flux or destablized, but that sexual orientation is itself a precariously constructed identity. I see it not as some fixed, essentialized characteristic of an individual, but as a socially, psychically and historically constructed phenomenon.

4. I am indebted to Ursula Kelly, Mount St. Vincent University, for naming the nexus of femininity, passivity, and pleasure, so clearly in discussions concerning this research.

5. It is important to point out that within the genre all women are, in part, defined in terms of their oppression within gendered relations of power. This is not to suggest that all women are uniformly oppressed or powerless. Class, race, and other social and contextual factors need to be considered.

6. The thesis on which this book is based was originally entitled "Danger at the Borders: The Response of High School Girls to Feminist Writing Practices." The terms *border* and *border-crossings* appear frequently in the area of critical pedagogy, most notably in the early work of Henry Giroux and more recently reconceptualized by Handel Kashope Wright (1995).

7. Sigmund Freud theorized the relationship between desire and identification in a number of his writings, for example, "New Introductory Lectures," vol. 22 and "Group Psychology and the Analysis of the Ego," vol. 18, in James Strachey's 1964, *The Standard Edition of the Complete Psychological Works of Sigmund Freud*, London: The Hogarth Press.

8. For an excellent discussion of Freud's assumption of an immature homosexual identity see Diana Fuss's chapter "'Fallen Women': The Psychogenesis of a Case of Homosexuality in a Woman" in her 1995 text *Identification Paper*, London, UK: Routledge.

9. English studies has been in a state of crisis over the past decade. Cultural Studies, Media Studies, Feminist and Postcolonial Theory are threatening more traditional orientations that have dominated the field. This text is obviously aligned with a Cultural Studies orientation as described by Morgan (1993, 2000), Piem (1990), and Bennett (1990).

10. *English Quarterly* 25 (1992), features reviews by Dennis Sumara, York University, of a number of gay and lesbian literary texts suitable for inclusion in the high school English Studies curriculum. The review includes Diana Wieler's novel *Bad Boy*, a text that won the Governor General's Award.

References

AAUW. 1995. *How Schools Shortchange Girls: The AAUW Report: A Study of Major Findings on Girls and Education.* New York: Marlow & Company.

Althusser, Louis. 1971. *Lenin and Philosophy and Other Essays.* New York: Left Books.

Anderson, Bonnie, and Judith Zinsser. 1988. *A History of Their Own: Women in Europe From Prehistory to the Present.* Vol. 2. New York: Harper and Row.

Anderson, Gary. 1989. Critical ethnography in education: Origins, current status, and new directions. *Review of Educational Research,* 59(3): 249–270.

Annas, Pamela. 1985. Style as politics: A Feminist approach to the teaching of writing. *College English,* 47(4): 360–370.

Ayim, Maryann Neely. 1997. *The Moral Parameters of Good Talk: A Feminist Analysis.* Waterloo, Ontario: Wilfrid Laurier University Press.

Barnes, Linda. 1990. Gender bias in teachers' written comments. In *Gender in the Classroom: Power and Pedagogy,* edited by Susan L. Gabriel and Isaiah Smithson. Chicago: University of Illinois Press, pp. 128–140.

Barthes, Roland. 1975. *The Pleasure of the Text.* New York: The Noonday Press.

Benjamin, Jessica. 1995. *Like Subjects, Love Objects: Essays on Recognition and Sexual Difference.* New Haven: Yale University Press.

————. 1988. *Bonds of Love: Psychoanalysis, Feminism and the Problem of Domination*. New York: Pantheon.

Bennett, Tony. 1990. *Outside Literature*. London: Routledge.

Bennett, Tony, and Janet Woollacott. 1987. *Bond and Beyond: The Political Career of a Popular Hero*. London: McMillan.

Bogdan, Deanne. 1994. When is a singing school (not) a chorus? The emancipatory agenda in feminist pedagogy and literature education. In The *Education Feminism Reader,* edited by Lynda Stone. London: Routledge Press, pp. 349–358.

Brand, Alice. 1980. Creative writing in English education: An historical perspective. *Journal of Education* 162(4): 63–83.

Brandt, Di. 1988. *(f.)Lip* 2(1): 20.

Britzman, Deborah. 1998. *Lost Subjects, Contested Objects: Toward a Psychoanalytic Inquiry of Learning*. Albany: State University of New York Press.

————. 1995. What is this thing called love? *Taboo* 1:63–93.

————. 1993. Beyond rolling models: Gender and multicultural education. In *Gender and Education*, edited by Sari K. Biklen and Diane Pollard. Chicago: University of Chicago Press, pp. 25–42.

Butler, Judith. 1997. Performative acts and gender constitution: An essay in phenomenology and feminist theory. In *Writing on the Body: Female Embodiment and Feminist Theory,* edited by Katie Conboy, Nadia Medina and Sarah Stanbury. New York: Columbia University Press, pp. 401–417.

————. 1993. *Bodies That Matter: On the Discursive Limits of "Sex."* New York: Routledge.

————. 1990. *Gender Trouble: Feminism and the Subversion of Identity*. New York: Routledge.

Cameron, Deborah, ed., 1998. *The Feminist Critique of Language: A Reader*, 2nd edition. London: Routledge.

Caywood, Cynthia, and Gillian Overing. 1987. *Teaching Writing: Pedagogy, Gender, and Equity*. Albany, NY: State University of New York Press.

Cherland, Meredith, Rogers. 1994. *Private Practices: Girls Reading Fiction and Constructing Identity*. London: Taylor and Francis.

Cherland, Meredith, Rogers, and Carole Edelsky. 1993. Girls and reading: The desire for agency and the horror of helplessness in fictional encounters. In *Texts of Desire: Essays on Fiction, Femininity, and Schooling*, edited by Linda Christian-Smith. London: The Falmer Press, pp. 28–44.

Cixous, Helene. 1980. The laugh of the medusa. In *New French Feminism: An Anthology*, edited by Elaine Marks and Isabelle de Courtivron. New York: Schocken Books, pp. 245–264.

Coates, Jennifer, ed. 1998. *Language and Gender: A Reader*. Oxford: Blackwell.

Corrigan, Philip. 1990. The making of the boy: Meditations on what grammar school did with, to, and for my body. In *Postmodernism Feminism and Cultural Politics*, edited by Henry Giroux. Albany: State University of New York Press, pp. 196–216.

Coulter, Rebecca. 1995. Struggling with sexism: Experiences of feminist first-year teachers. *Gender and Education* 7(1): 33–50.

Crowley, Sharon. 1989. *A Teacher's Introduction to Deconstruction*. Urbana Illinois: NCTE.

Davies, Bronwyn. 1990. The problem of desire. *Social Problems,* 37 (4): 501–516.

———. 1989. The discursive production of the male/female dualism in school settings. *Oxford Review of Education* 15(3): 229–241.

Davies, Bronwyn, and Chas Banks. 1992. The gender trap: a feminist poststructuralist analysis of primary school children's talk about gender. *Journal of Curriculum Studies* 24(1): 1–25.

Davis, Hilary. 1993. Recuperating pleasure: Towards a Feminist aesthetic of reading. Ph. diss. Toronto: The Ontario Institute for Studies in Education.

de Castell, Suzanne, Allan Luke, and Kieran Egan. 1986. *Literacy, Society and Schooling: A Reader.* New York: Cambridge University Press.

de Lauretis, Teresa. 1986. *Feminist Studies/Critical Studies.* Bloomington: Indiana University Press.

Deem, Rosemary. 1980. *Schooling for Women's Work.* London, UK: Routledge, Keagan, Paul.

Dewey, John. 1938. *Education and Experience.* Lasalle, IL: Open Court Press.

Easton, Alison. 1989. With her in ourland: A feminist teaches nineteenth-century American literature. In *Teaching Women: Feminism and English Studies,* edited by Ann Thompson and Helen Wilcox. Manchester: Manchester University Press, pp. 149–160.

Faludi, Susan. 1992. *Backlash: The Undeclared War Against American Women.* New York: Doubleday.

Felman, Shosana. 1982. Psychoanalysis and education: Teaching terminable and interminable. *Yale French Studies* 63: 21–43.

Fetterly, Judith. 1978. *The Resisting Reader.* Bloomington: Indiana University Press.

Fine, Michelle, and Pat Macpherson. 1992. Over dinner: Feminism and adolescent female bodies. In *Disruptive Voices: The Possibilities of Feminist Research,* edited by Michelle Fine. Ann Arbour: The University of Michigan Press, pp. 175–203.

Finke, Laurie. 1996. Knowledge as Bait: Feminism, Voice, and the Pedagogical Unconscious. In *Learning Desire: Perspectives on*

Pedagogy, Culture and the Unsaid, edited by Sharon Todd. New York: Routledge, pp. 117–140.

Flax, Jane. 1990. *Thinking Fragments: Psychoanalysis, Feminism, and Postmodernism in the Contemporary West.* Berkeley: University of California Press.

Foucault, Michel. 1981. *The History of Sexuality, Vol. 1: An Introduction.* Harmondsworth: Pelican Press.

Freud, Anna. 1971. *The Writings of Anna Freud. Vol. 7: Problems of Psychoanalytic Training, Diagnosis, and the Technique of Therapy: 1966–1970.* New York: International University Press.

Freud, Sigmund. 1964a. Group Psychology and the Analysis of the Ego. In *The Standard Edition of the Complete Psychological Works of Sigmund Freud.* Vol. 18, edited by James Strachey. London: Hogarth.

———. 1964b. New Introductory Lectures. In *The Standard Edition of the Complete Psychological Works of Sigmund Freud.* Vol. 22, edited by James Strachey. London: Hogarth.

Friedman, Ellen, and Miriam Fuchs. 1989. *Breaking the Sequence: Women's Experimental Fiction.* Princeton: Princeton University Press.

Frith, Gill. 1981. Little women, good wives: Is English good for girls? In *Feminism for Girls: An Adventure Story,* edited by Angela McRobbie and Mira Nava. London: Routledge & Keagan Paul, Press, pp. 26–49.

Fuss, Diane. 1995. *Identification Papers.* New York: Routledge.

Gallop, Jane. 1995. *Pedagogy: The Question of Impersonation.* Bloomington: Indiana University Press.

———. 1993. The institutionalizing of feminist criticism. In *English Inside and Out: The Places of Literary Criticism,* edited by Susan Gubar and J. Kamholtz. New York: Routledge Press, pp. 61–67.

Galloway, Patricia. 1980. *What's Wrong with High School English? It's Sexist, UnCanadian, Outdated.* Toronto: The Ontario Institute for Studies in Education Press.

Gaskell, Jane and Arlene McLaren. 1989. *Women and Education: A Canadian Perspective.* Calgary, Alberta: Detselig.

Gilbert, Pam. 1992. The story so far: Gender, literacy and social regulation. *Gender and Education* 4(3): 185–199.

―――. 1991. From voice to text: Reconsidering writing and reading in the English classroom. *English Education* 23(4): 195–211.

―――. 1989a. Student text as pedagogical text. In *Language, Authority and Criticism: Readings on the School Textbook,* edited by Suzanne de Castell, Allan Luke, and Carmen Luke. New York: Falmer Press, pp. 195–202.

―――. 1989b. Personally (and passively) yours: Girls, literacy, and education. *Oxford Review of Education* 15: 257–265.

―――. 1988. Stoning the romance: Girls as resistant readers and writers. *Curriculum Perspectives* 8(2): 13–18.

Gilbert, Susan, and Sandra Gubar. 1984. *The Madwoman in the Attic: The Woman Writer and Nineteenth Century Literary Imagination.* New Haven: Yale University Press.

Gilligan, Carol. 1990. *Making Connections: The Relational Worlds of Adolescent Girls at Emma Willard School.* Cambridge: Harvard University Press.

Globe and Mail (February 10, 1993). Sweet Sixteen. A16.

Gould, Karen. 1990. *Writing in the Feminine: Feminism and Experimental Writing in Quebec.* Carbondale: Southern Illinois University Press.

Grossberg, Lawrence. 1986. Teaching the popular. In *Theory in the Classroom*, edited by Cary Nelson. Urbana: University of Illinois Press, pp. 177–199.

Harding, Sandra. 1987. *Feminism and Methodology.* Bloomington: Indiana University Press.

Harper, Helen. 1998. Dangerous desires: Feminist literary criticism in high school Writing class. *Theory Into Practice* 37(3): 220–228.

――――. 1997. Disturbing identity and desire: Adolescent girls and wild words. In *Learning Desire: Perspectives on Pedagogy, Culture and the Unsaid,* edited by Sharon Todd. New York: Routledge, pp. 140–161.

――――. 1996. Reading, identity and desire: High school girls and feminist avant-garde literature. *Journal of Curriculum Theorizing,* 12(4): 6–13.

Hudson, Barbara. 1984. Femininity and adolescence. In *Gender and Generation,* edited by Angela McRobbie and Miriam Nava, Baskingstoke: Macmillan, pp. 31–53.

Irigaray, Luce. 1971. *The Sex Which Is Not One.* Ithaca: Cornell University Press.

Jones, Alison. 1997. Teaching post-structuralist feminist theory in education: Student resistances. *Gender and Education,* 9(3): 261–269.

――――. 1993. Becoming a "Girl": Post-structuralist suggestions for educational research. *Gender and Education,* 5(2): 157–166.

Junker, Clara. 1988. Writing (With) Cixous. *College English,* 50(4): 424–436.

Kaplan, Cora. 1991. Gender and Language. In *The Feminist Critique of Language: A Reader,* edited by Deborah Cameron. New York: Routledge, pp. 54–64.

Kelly, Ursula. 1997. *Schooling Desire: Literacy, Cultural Politics, and Pedagogy.* New York: Routledge.

King, Katie. 1986. The situation of lesbianism as Feminism's magical sign: Contests for meaning and U.S. Women's movement, 1968–1972. *Communications* 9(1): 65–91.

Lakoff, Robin. 1975. *Language and Women's Place.* New York: Harper and Row.

Larkin, June. 1997. Confronting sexual harassment in schools. *Orbit* 28(1): 14–15.

———. 1994. *Sexual Harassment: High School Girls Speak Out.* Toronto: Second Story Press.

Lather, Patti. 1991. *Getting Smart: Feminist Research and Pedagogy With/in the Postmodern.* London: Routledge.

Lesko, Nancy. 1988. The curriculum of the body: Lessons from a Catholic high school. In *Becoming Feminine: The Politics of Popular Culture,* edited by Leslie Roman, Linda Christian-Smith, and Elizabeth Ellsworth. London: Falmer Press, pp. 123–141.

Mathieson, Margaret. 1975. *Preachers of Culture.* London: Allen & Unwin.

McLaren, Peter. 1990. Schooling the postmodern body: Critical pedagogy and the politics of enfleshment. In *Postmodernism, Feminism and Cultural Politics,* edited by Henry Giroux. Albany: State University of New York Press.

McRobbie, Angela. 1992. From Jackie to Just Seventeen: Girls' magazines in the 1980s. In *Feminism and Youth Culture: From Jackie to Just Seventeen,* edited by Angela McRobbie. London: Macmillan, pp. 135–189.

Middleton, Sue, and Alison Jones. 1992. *Women and Education in Aotearoa.* Wellington: Bridget Williams Books.

Morgan, Robert. 2000. Uncertain relations: English and Cultural studies. In *Advocating Change: Contemporary Issues in Subject English,* edited by B. Barrell and R. Hammett. Toronto: Irwin Press, pp. 14–34.

———. 1993. Transitions from English to Cultural Studies. *New Education* 15(1): 21–48.

————. 1987. Three dreams of language: Or, no longer immured in the bastille of the humanist word. *College English,* 49(4): 449–458.

Morton, Donald, and Mas'ud Zavarzadeh. 1991. *Texts for Change: Theory/Pedagogy/Politics.* Chicago: University of Illinois Press.

Nin, Anais. 1967. *The Diary of Anais Nin.* New York: Swallow Press.

O'Neill, Marnie. 1992. Teaching Literature as cultural criticism. *English Quarterly* 25(1): 19–25.

Otte, George. 1995. In-Voicing: Beyond the voice debate. In *Pedagogy: The Question of Impersonation,* edited by Jane Gallop. Bloomington: Indiana University Press, pp. 147–154.

Piem, Nick. 1990. *English Teaching and Critical Theory.* London: Routledge.

Piercy, Marge. 1976. *Women on the Edge of Time.* New York: Fawcrett.

Pitt, Alice. 1996. Fantasizing women in the women's studies classroom: Toward a symptomatic reading of negation. *Journal of Curriculum Theorizing* 12(4): 32–40.

Prince, Heather. 1987. The Creationist. *(f.)Lip* 1(3): 11.

Rich, Adrienne. 1980. Compulsory heterosexuality and lesbian existence. In *Women, Sex and Sexuality,* edited by Catherine Simpson and E. Person. Chicago: University of Chicago Press, pp. 652–691.

Robertson, Judith. 1997a. Screenplay pedagogy and the interpretation of unexamined knowledge in pre-service primary teaching. *Taboo* 1(Spring): 25–60.

————. 1997b. Popular culture and the education of the female primary-school teacher. In *Learning Desire: Perspectives on Pedagogy, Culture and the Unsaid,* edited by Sharon Todd. New York: Routledge, pp. 75–95.

————. 1994. Cinema and the Politics of Desire in Teacher Education. Ph.D. diss. The Ontario Institute for Studies in Education. Toronto, Ontario.

Russ, Joanna. 1975. *The Female Man.* Boston: Beacon Press.

Sadker, Myra, and David Sadker. 1994. *Failing at Fairness: How American Schools Cheat Girls.* New York: Scribner.

Schulz, Muriel. 1991. The semantic derogation of woman. In *Feminist Critique of Language*, first edition, edited by Deborah Cameron. London: Routledge, pp. 134–147.

Scott, Gail. 1989. *Spaces Like Stairs.* Toronto: Women's Press.

Simon, Roger. 1992. *Teaching Against the Grain: Texts for a Pedagogy of Possibility.* Toronto: OISE Press.

Smith, Dorothy. 1987. *The Everyday World as Problematic: A Feminist Sociology.* Boston: Northeastern University Press.

Spender, Dale. 1980. *Man Made Language.* London: Routledge.

Spender, Dale, and Elizabeth Sarah. 1980. *Learning to Lose: Sexism and Education.* London: Writings and Readers Publishing Cooperative.

Stein, N., N. Marshall, and L. Tropp. 1993. Secrets in public: Sexual harassment in our schools. Wellesley, MA: Centre for Research on Women at Wellesley College and the NOW Legal Defense and Education Fund.

Sumara, Dennis. 1992. Gay and lesbian voices in literature: Making room on the shelf. *English Quarterly* 25(1): 30–34.

The Telling It Book Collective, ed. 1990. *Telling It: Woman and Language Across Cultures.* Vancouver: Press Gang.

Tregebov, Rhea. 1987. *Work in Progress: Building Feminist Culture.* Toronto: The Women's Press.

Trinh, Minh-Ha. 1992. *Framer Framed*. New York: Routledge.

Walkerdine, Valerie. 1990. *Schoolgirl Fictions*. London: Verso Press.

————. 1987. Some day my prince will come. In *Gender and Generation*, edited by Angela McRobbie and Miriam Nava. London: Macmillan, pp. 162–168.

Waring, Wendy. 1987. Strategies for subversion: Canadian women's writing. In *Work in Progress*, edited by Rhea Tregebov. Toronto: The Women's Press, pp. 7–13.

Warland, Betsy. 1993. 'a language that holds us.' In *Sounding Differences: Conversations with Seventeen Canadian Women Writers*, edited by Janice Williamson. Toronto: University of Toronto Press, pp. 303–315.

Warner, Michael. 1993. *Fear of a Queer Planet: Queer Politics and Social Theory*. Minneapolis: University of Minnesota Press.

Weedon, Chris. 1997. *Feminist Practice and Poststructuralist Theory*, 2nd edition. Oxford: Blackwell.

Williamson, Janice. 1993. *Sounding Differences: Conversations with Seventeen Canadian Women Writers*. Toronto: University of Toronto Press.

Wittig, Monique. 1990. The straight mind. In *Out There: Marginalization and Contemporary Cultures,* edited by Russell Ferguson, Martha Gever, Trinh Minh-Ha, and Cornel West. Cambridge: MIT Press, pp. 51–57.

Wolff, Janet. 1991. Writing passionately: Student resistance to feminist readings. *College Composition and Communication* 42(4): 484–492.

Woolf, Virgina. 1984. *Women and Writing*. Toronto: University of Toronto Press.

Wright, Handel, K. 1995. (Re)Conceptualizing pedagogy as cultural praxis. *Education and Society* 13(1): 67–81.

Appendix
Literature Studied in the Project

Allen, Lillian. 1982. "I Fight Back." *Fireweed* 14 (Fall): 27.

Bernikow, L. 1980. "Mother-Daughter Fights." In *Among Women,* by Louise Bernikow. New York: Crown Publishers.

Duncan, Francis. 1987. "PATTERN MAKERS." *(f.)Lip* (3): 10.

Geauvreau, Cherie. 1987. "Straw Doll." *(f.)Lip* (1): 11–12.

Harjo, Joy. 1984. "I am a Dangerous Woman." In *That's What She Said*, edited by Rayna Green. Bloomington: Indiana University Press, pp. 128–129.

Hryniuk, Angela. 1990. "the hairdresser." *Fireweed* 31 (Fall): 101.

Kealey, Susan. 1990. "stairwell home." (referred to as "The Bag-lady Poem" in the study) *Fireweed* 31 (Fall): 86.

Larson, Jacqueline. 1988. "A Sight." *(f.)Lip* (4): 11–12.

Malkin, Anna. 1990. "The Fall." *Fireweed* 31(Fall): 37.

Murray, Carla. 1990. "I Saw a Monster." *Fireweed* 31(Fall): 96.

Nourbese Philip, M. 1987. "Discourse on the Logic of Language." *(f.)Lip* (1): 21–25.

Oka, Noriko. 1990. "the portrait." *Fireweed* 32 (Spring): 105.

Onyshack, Ursula. 1990. "Feminist Weekend." *Contemporary Verse* 13, (Winter): 27.

Oughton, L. 1988. "so i'm afraid of getting what i want?" *(f.)Lip* (2): 12.

Parks, Joy. 1987. "Rhymes to Grow By." Fireweed 9 (Fall): 97–101.

Wallace, Bronwen. 1987. "Between Words (for Carole)." *Fireweed* 9 (Winter): 34–36.

————. 1983. "The Woman in This Poem." In *Signs of the Former Tenant,* by Bronwen Wallace. Ottawa: Oberon Press, p. 19.

Yee May. 1990. "Chinese Landscapes." *Fireweed* 32 (Spring): 65.

Young, Patricia. 1988. "Passmore Street." *(f.)Lip* (4): 4–7.

Studies in the Postmodern Theory of Education

General Editors
Joe L. Kincheloe & Shirley R. Steinberg

Counterpoints publishes the most compelling and imaginative books being
written in education today. Grounded on the theoretical advances in
criticalism, feminism, and postmodernism in the last two decades of the
twentieth century, Counterpoints engages the meaning of these innovations
in various forms of educational expression. Committed to the proposition
that theoretical literature should be accessible to a variety of audiences, the
series insists that its authors avoid esoteric and jargonistic languages that
transform educational scholarship into an elite discourse for the initiated.
Scholarly work matters only to the degree it affects consciousness and
practice at multiple sites. Counterpoints' editorial policy is based on these
principles and the ability of scholars to break new ground, to open new
conversations, to go where educators have never gone before.

For additional information about this series or for the submission of
manuscripts, please contact:

> Joe L. Kincheloe & Shirley R. Steinberg
> 637 West Foster Avenue
> State College, PA 16801

To order other books in this series, please contact our Customer Service
Department at:

> (800) 770-LANG (within the U.S.)
> (212) 647-7706 (outside the U.S.)
> (212) 647-7707 FAX

or browse online by series at:

> www.peterlang.com